WITHDRAWN

DRAMA IN RELIGIOUS EDUCATION
A Teacher's Handbook

DRAMA IN
RELIGIOUS EDUCATION

A Teacher's Handbook

Victor J. Green
B.A., L.G.S.M. (*Speech and Drama*)

BLANDFORD PRESS
Poole   Dorset

First published in the U.K. 1979

Copyright © 1979 Blandford Press Ltd,
Link House, West Street,
Poole, Dorset, BH15 1LL

British Library Cataloguing in Publication Data

Green, Victor J
  Drama in religious education.
  1. Drama in religious education
  I. Title
  200'.7'8   BV1534.4

ISBN 0 7137 0983 9

Set in 10/11 Sabon, printed and bound in Great Britain by
Butler & Tanner Ltd, Frome and London

Contents

Acknowledgements

Acknowledgement is due to Macmillan Publishing Co. Inc, New York, for permission to include the narrative poem *The Daniel Jazz* by Vachel Lindsay; and to J. M. Dent & Sons Ltd for permission to base my section *Mediaeval Plays for Christmas* on material in their Everyman volume *Everyman: with other interludes*; to George G. Harrap & Co Ltd for permission to draw material from *The Goalkeeper's Revenge – and other stories* by Bill Naughton in the section *Spit Nolan*, and to the literary executor of the late Romesh Dutt for my section *The Ramayana* which is derived from the translation of his narrative poem *The Ramayana and Mahabharata*.

My personal thanks are also due to the following for giving generously of time and helpful information; Suresh C. Khatri (for *The Mystery of the Well*), Mrs Joan Ticer (for *Treatment of Materials*), Mrs Barbara Wills (for suggestions for *Improvisation*), Mr Terence Goldsmith of Blandford Press, and to all the many young people and teachers who have worked with me in the development of most of the material in this book. In particular I am indebted to my wife who has once more translated my near-indecipherable manuscript into the neatest of typescript.

VICTOR J. GREEN

Foreword

One of the oldest precepts in Education is that we learn by doing, and this is true at all stages. Drama is doing, playing out events, ideas, emotions and relationships. Dramatic work involves elements of speaking, writing, mime, movement, prose, poetry, music, dance, art, dress and lighting. There are many books, only a fraction of which are listed at the back of this book, designed to help a teacher in this work. It would obviously be impossible to put everything on this subject between the covers of one book. *Drama in Religious Education* is for the teacher or leader with young people between the ages of about eight to thirteen years who feels impelled to include dramatic work in its widest sense but who is reluctant to attempt it, through a lack of experience or uncertainty about suitable material.

The first part gives, as simply as possible, general suggestions about presentation. The greater part of the book is devoted to dramatic material, with synopses of dance, mime and dramatic work, including scripts and unscripted drama, covering classroom work as well as work suitable for presenting to an audience. Much of the work reflects Christian belief and comment on it, but there is also some material drawn from stories and incidents from other faiths.

In all this work simplicity is vital, for over-elaborate staging and costume or over-ambitious production may well detract from the impact of its intention.

Most of the suggestions have been worked through by the author, either with young people of the appropriate age group or by teachers attending courses in Religious Drama. It is not possible to attach any particular age group to each piece of work; much will depend on the teacher's experience, the teacher's knowledge of the capability of his or her own group and principally on the experience of the young people themselves.

The material has been arranged rather arbitrarily in order of suitability from the youngest to the oldest in the age groupings the book is concerned with, but it is unlikely that there will be general agreement about this. Some of the pieces can be attempted by teacher and class with little experience, while the material towards the end of the book requires a group of young people with experience of dance and mime.

A teacher of Drama must be a magpie for material, looking out for poems, stories, newspaper items, radio and TV programmes to provide inspiration for dramatic work. Look out constantly for pieces of music or sounds which might provide a background for a mood or incident which forms part of classroom or presentation drama.

I hope that the material will demonstrate for itself that Religious Drama does not have to be solemn or necessarily contain great moral messages. Sometimes it will contain a teaching element but generally the work will deal with relationships, our interdependence, and the histories, stories and legends through which religious experience has been built up. The value of much of the work suggested will be in the discussion that goes on around it and the development of the themes in classroom dialogue.

Finally a teacher need have no anxieties about seeming to do no more than imitate, for the impact of any piece of work will depend largely on the relationships between teacher and the group, and because of this the end result will bear its individual stamp.

Their involvement was complete and they learned so much from each other.

When playing in arena try to avoid actors standing for any length of time close to the audience. Such a player blots out everything from the sight of a section of the onlookers. Contrive that such players sit or kneel and concentrate rather on 'pyramid' grouping, the dominant players focussed towards the centre, possibly on rostra. The actors in arena form must be trained to 'whole body' acting, acting with their backs as well as with their facial expression. An actor who is angry, for instance, has to appear to be angry both to an audience facing him as well as an audience behind him.

For those with very limited space, I would suggest experimentation with tableaux to music, prose or poetry. Discuss at length the piece of work to be attempted, allot lines to individuals, small groups and the whole group. Build up an impressive grouping with figures lying, sitting, standing, and yet allow as much gesture, movement, turning heads towards a speaker and so on. Make every gesture, every movement of head, hand and body, meaningful. It is possible to achieve effects of wind, rain, storm, sunshine, moods, strengths and weaknesses. For classroom work start with something simple like a psalm or a small excerpt from the Bible, as for instance the Sermon on the Mount. I have seen an experienced group of twelve to thirteen-year-olds speak and perform *God's Grandeur* by Gerard Manley Hopkins, but this is not one to start with.

In all this work emphasise the use of eyes and eye lines. Two people talking to each other can strengthen the attention and interest of the audience by the intensity of their looking, just as an avoidance of a look can say a great deal. There are few things that can douse the attention of an audience so much as one of the actors looking around, disinterested in what is going on in the arena. The audience will invariably follow his eye-line to see what he is looking at.

The medieval religious drama was centred around the cycles of mystery plays and, with suitable adaptation, these are well within the ability of the age group with which we are concerned. They have a directness of speech which appeals to young people. They were often played on waggons which moved from one part of the village to another. The audience stayed at each of the stations while scene after scene came to them to be presented. It appears that occasionally the audience moved from station to station, rather in the fashion used for the 'Stations of the Cross' in the Catholic Church, the worshippers move round the church following the fourteen 'stations' or 'representations' of Jesus' journey along the Way of the Cross to His crucifixion.

Quite recently I saw this method used by the children of the village school at Standlake in Oxfordshire on the occasion of the 800th anniversary of the founding of the church.

They used five flat farm waggons which were stationed around the field in which the celebration took place. Five episodes in the life of the church and village were dramatised by a member of staff and simple scenes were set up on the waggons to back the action. The five groups of players, suitably costumed, waited at the back of each waggon and acted out the foundation of the church, eight hundred years before, and other events that had taken place through the years. Had the players spoken the words as they acted, the sound would have been lost and to use a microphone at each station would have presented problems. The players had, in fact, carefully recorded the dialogue previously in the classroom and the tape was amplified so that the words were heard all over the field. At the end of the first scene, the audience moved on to the second station and so on to the end of the pageant. A very imaginative presentation using modern invention with medieval material.

This technique could be used effectively in conjunction with tableaux vivants accompanied by recorded voices or with talk-over from a microphone. Those who have seen the Passion Play at Oberammergau will appreciate that this method is used for the tableaux on the inner stage, while more conventional dramatic scenes are played on the open stage.

Church schools will probably want to use the church for productions and this is obviously to be encouraged, with a few words of warning. It is notoriously difficult to see what is going on in the chancel of churches particularly if the ends of the pews are adorned with 'poppy heads'.

The most successful presentations in churches with which I have been concerned have made some attempt to put a sort of staging either in the chancel or in the crossing between the transepts. On one occasion we put boards right across the tops of the choir stalls with a central support. A staging in the transept with steps up in front and behind has proved successful. In any case make use of the features of the church itself. Entrances can be made from the font right down the centre of the church. If the centre aisle is wide, use it for some of the scenes and certainly use the pulpit or side chapels if at all possible. If your play has a commentator or reader, the pulpit is an obvious position for him.

In church productions even more attention must be paid to speech and use of voice, and it is essential to rehearse in the church rather than to hold rehearsals at school and face the problems presented by church performances too late to do anything about them.

Costume

What Shall We Wear?

For classroom work and, for the most part, for assembly presentations, costume will not be an issue, but for more finished work designed to show to an audience, costume will be something to be considered. Once more, simplicity is to be aimed at. The work of young people will be poorer if the costume they wear is elaborate and unusual. I have seen Nativity Plays by quite young people, even infants, in which some players are clad like biblical Palestinians and Victorian angels, together with other players on all fours pretending to be donkeys and oxen. It is more effective to give an impression of character by using a simple token piece of costume over the player's normal clothing than it is to try to create a full-scale outfit. Movement is so much easier and more natural if the young player is wearing clothes to which he or she is accustomed. In the instance quoted above, the shepherds need no more than a blanket around the shoulders, the kings need a simple coronet, while angels could be recognised by a simple white or silver sash. There would then be no difficulty in mounting steps, bowing or kneeling.

In many plays, simple masks will be sufficient to denote animal characters, allowing the player to indicate movement whilst maintaining an upright posture. Young people, or old ones for that matter, look ridiculous when trying to act four-legged creatures on all fours. Another way in which such characters can be contrived is to allow the player to carry a device on a short stick to indicate an animal character or a divine character or indeed any character for which there are problems in costume design. Audiences are very quick to accept such conventions and appreciate originality and ingenuity.

For most of the items involving dance, mime and pure movement, the body should be as free as possible and the most appropriate garment is the leotard, or any other such dress allowing complete freedom for body, arms and legs.

Even so there will be times when some sort of costume is called for and it will be found possible to design costumes from two basic shapes, a rectangle or a square, regarded as a diamond for this purpose.

The rectangle will be long or short in proportion to the width as the costume requires. The patterns are cut with a slit through which the player's head goes, as shown in the diagram.

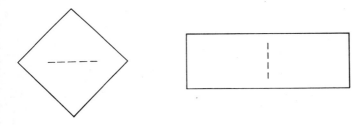

With the head going through the slit the rectangle will fall back and front of the player and can be pulled together round the waist with a sash. This makes a 'dress' costume of whatever length is required. Collars or scarves will fill in round the neck. The diamond-shaped costume will fall like a 'poncho' over the player's body and again can be pulled together with a sash or left free. If the play involves animals and birds these basic costumes can be cut to indicate animal skins or birds' feathers.

The basic material can be treated by dyeing or printing to be more effective.

FABRIC PRINTING

Dyeing and decorating fabrics is one of the oldest arts of mankind and ancient simple techniques continue to produce fascinating and effective results. For the purpose of this book three techniques are suggested: Block printing, Tie and Dye, and Batik.

BLOCK PRINTING

This process is carried out by using raised surfaces made by cutting into the block of material used, which can be potato, wood or lino, while other interesting designs can be made from items found about the house which have ready-made raised surfaces, such as buttons, corks, coins and so on.

To start with a potato block, cut a triangular or oblong block from a large clean potato. Cut the required simple pattern into the potato surface, avoiding thin ridges which will easily break down. The printing surfaces should protrude by about 64 cm ($\frac{1}{4}$ inch), so that when the pattern surface becomes worn it can be renewed by cutting a little away. Before inking, the block should be firmly pressed a few times on to absorbent paper so as to remove excess moisture. The block is coated with permanent ink by means of a brush, and then pressed firmly and evenly on the fabric. Before printing, the fabric should be washed, rinsed and dried to remove any dressing it may contain. The block is used again and again until the area is covered with the design.

TIE-AND-DYE

Tie-and-Dye or tie-dyeing is a resist-dyeing process. It consists of knotting, binding, folding or sewing some parts of the fabric in such a way that when it is dyed, the dye cannot penetrate into these areas.

The cloth to be dyed must first be washed to remove any dressing it may contain. The pattern can be marked out on the fabric in pencil. This does not involve complicated patterns but rather designated areas of colour or lack of colour. The material is then prepared by knotting, binding, folding and so on or by a combination of these techniques. Various effects can be achieved:

Sunbursts: Indicate circles of various sizes. Pick up the fabric at the point you wish to make the centre of the pattern, so that the material resembles a furled umbrella and then bind tightly at intervals according to the required size of circles.

Knotting: Fold the material into a strip and knot it at regular intervals.

Pleating: Fold the fabric into a narrow strip of accordion pleats and bind at regular intervals.

Marbling: Crumple up the fabric into a ball and bind with string before dyeing. Untie and crumble again and then bind up again with string before dyeing with another colour.

When the material has been prepared by whatever technique you choose, wet the material and place in the dye for the period of time recommended by the dye manufacturer. Remove from the dye bath and squeeze out the surplus dye. Rinse in cold water until the water is clear of colour, squeeze out surplus water and hang up to dry. When a second or third colour is to be dyed, tie up the cloth again or add more binding where the previous colour is to be retained. Repeat the dyeing process for each colour. After the final dyeing and rinsing, dry as quickly as possible. Untie the fabric, rinse again if necessary and partially dry. Iron while still damp.

BATIK

Batik is the Javanese name for one of the oldest and most widespread ways of decorating fabric known to man. Javanese Batik has become so famous that the name is now given to all fabrics decorated in this way, wherever they have been made.

The conventional method is described first but it must be used with great care and younger children should use the second and less hazardous method described.

The pattern on the material is made by painting the design on with very hot liquid wax before immersing the whole in a dye bath. It will be clear that young pupils attempting this will need close supervision. The wax prevents the dye reaching the painted pattern and the finished material is left with a pale pattern on a coloured ground. The dye bath has to be cold, otherwise the wax would melt. The wax can be deliberately cracked so that a fine spider web effect can be achieved by the dye seeping into the cracks.

After dyeing and drying, the wax has to be removed. This can be done by cracking very thick wax and working the fabric with the hands. The remainder can be ironed out by placing the fabric between several sheets of newspaper or tissue paper. Should the wax prove difficult to remove, the fabric may be boiled in water containing pure soap flakes, rinsed thoroughly in hot water and then finally in cold water.

For a teacher with any doubts about using this technique involving hot molten wax, there is a simpler method which avoids this hazard.

FLOUR AND WATER RESIST

In this method the resist is made from a flour paste. Use plain flour with a little salt added to prevent deterioration. Add sufficient water to make a mixture with the consistency of thick cream, slightly thicker than double cream. Apply this creamy mixture with a brush or spoon or pipe it on from a squeezy bottle. This will follow the pattern or design required on the material. Whereas with the hot wax method the material is immersed in a dye bath, with this flour and water resist method the dye is brushed on and allowed to dry. When the dyed material is dry, remove the resist by cracking the hard flour paste and working it off with the hands. What will not come away by hand can be removed by washing the fabric in cold water.

Movement

No work in drama will be effective or satisfying without basic work in movement. Movement involves control from finger tips to the ends of the toes and does not always mean lots of space although work will be limited if the students never have the opportunity to explore movement in relatively unconfined space.

Start in the classroom with the young people sitting at their desks or tables. With elbow resting on the desk, move the hand in circles from the wrist. Vary the speed at which the hand turns, vary the position of the fingers, try to get expression from the hand itself, make it soothing, make it menacing, make it ask questions, make it ugly, make it beautiful and so on. This simple exercise, with experience, can be developed into a drama of Good versus Evil. The two hands represent these characteristics in a dramatic conflict, the approach, the recognition, the threat, the struggle, the victory. Add suitable music, recorded or home-made, and there is drama. The students can then discuss how they felt, how the whole body seemed to be influenced by the moods and the conflict.

Hands can also be used to touch items, imaginary boxes, weighty objects, precious objects, live creatures, insects, and again little stories can be acted out by the hands. Here is one example:

Take down, from a shelf above, a heavy bottle of sweets. Unscrew the lid, put the lid down, take out a sweet wrapped in paper, unwrap the sweet, be careful what you do with the paper, chew the sweet, put back the screw top of the bottle, put the bottle back on the shelf.

When the opportunity arises to utilise more floor space make up 'conflict' exercises. Pair off the youngsters and, in turn, to drum beat or rattle, first one pushes back the other, then reverse the role and each in turn is submissive or superior. All this must be done without the actors touching each other. More experienced students will perform this exercise with space between them. This sort of exercise will be useful when performing such mimes as that in *The Good Samaritan*. In this, the arena is full of the attackers, hitting, punching, knifing and kicking with no player within touching distance of another player.

Whole body movements can be introduced with an exercise involving movement within a distance of 3 or 3.6 metres (10 or 12 feet). Suggest that an object, say an important letter, is lying on the ground about 3.6 metres (4 yards) away. First the group are told to go and pick it up. Then with the same situation they must cross thick, heavy mud to pick it up. The action is varied by crossing deep sand, a narrow mountain pass, a stony beach in bare feet, across a plank from one high building to another, or some other similar situation which can be contrived.

There is no room here to suggest a complete course in movement but these are the lines to work on until the groups can appreciate feeling right out to their finger tips.

Most of these exercises involve building up tension and then allowing it to flow away into relaxation.

With experience the group will be able to act out a story as it is read aloud. For instance, the story can begin with each player stretched out in the sun at the foot of a hill. He decides to climb the hill. At first the weather keeps fine but clouds spring up, the wind starts to blow, the rain falls and a thunderstorm breaks. The player battles his way on until he finds a little shed, the door is jammed, it needs all his strength to burst it open and then the player falls full length into the shelter of the hut.

Within these exercises evolve such themes as growing, climbing, falling, joy, sadness, threat, mystery and so on.

Miming stories will follow from this, involving groups of students, the stories being read aloud by some of the group and acted out in dumbshow by the others. In this book *The Daniel Jazz* is offered as an example. This poem sounds very modern in the same vein as *Joseph and his Technicolour Dreamcoat*, but is really much older. I used this with a group of thirteen-year-olds as long ago as 1946!

Improvisation, although a skill in its own right, may also be used as a bridge between mime and play acting. The real skill of the teacher is in finding a subject which will stimulate imagination and which will express itself in acting out the mood or situation expressed in the improvisation. The members of the class may decide for themselves whether to use words or not. Generally the better work is done 'without utterance', as the examination syllabus would put it.

In general this sort of work is for the upper end of the age range we are concerned with. Some subjects I have found to provoke imaginative responses are, 'The Intruder', 'The Bottle', 'The Mask', 'The Treasure Chest', 'Surrounded', 'Encounter of the Third Kind', 'Foggy Day', 'The Maze'.

Dance is a term to which some boys might object as being effeminate and not for them, so the word must be used carefully when the group is relatively inexperienced in mime and movement. I recall some difficulty when, for a teachers' course in one of the less favoured areas, I asked for a class of top juniors to help me in a demonstration, and the teacher informed the class before I arrived that a gentleman was coming to teach them to dance. I found that some resistance had to be broken down before we really found some rapport. Definitions in this work are difficult and the edges of the meanings of words like movement, dance, mime and so on are very blurred. Mime is generally taken to be action designed to create an illusion, while dance is a more structural movement designed to tell a story or express a mood. Often the subject itself suggests the treatment.

Genesis and Nativity, and *Away in a Manger* seem to me to be dance and mime. Hence my title of *Dance-Mime*. There are moods to express within a framework of a message-theme. The structure of these two works is important in the performance. Generally, dance is more rhythmic and is often accompanied by music, words or by mere rhythm, clapping, drumming or using other percussion instruments.

Some teachers of movement recommend complete spontaneity to be the only way, allowing free movement from the students in response to words, rhythms, music and so on, but I have generally found that for young people of any age being introduced to the work, some structure on the part of the teacher is an advantage, so long as the teacher avoids the

'You do it like this' situation. This can only lead to mimicry which inhibits individual response.

Perhaps it could be argued that mime is the only branch of drama that needs an audience since its success depends on creating an illusion in the mind of the onlooker. Following the exercises for hands described above, mime will need whole body reaction rather than response merely by hands. To greedy hands the performer must add greedy face, greedy arms, greedy eyes, greedy stance and greedy movement. The same applies for fear, surprise, joy, and so on. From time to time it is wise to allow the performers to be themselves and walk naturally.

An essential element in body control is relaxation. All exercises or activities requiring tension of any sort must be followed by relaxation exercises. These are fundamental in any aspect of drama.

Design

Lighting and Sets

For the greater part of the work in this book, classroom work, assemblies and most of the work for in-school consumption, there will be no need for lighting and not a great deal of complicated sets. However, the students at the senior end of the age range we are considering will sometimes prepare work for invited audiences and inevitably an interest in lighting is aroused and should be encouraged.

To light a centre arena, a square or rectangle of metal rods or piping is needed fixed to ceiling above the playing space with at least four, dependent on size of the arena, 500-watt Fresnel spotlights clamped to it. This must be considered a minimum to cover a small arena. Fresnel spots are adjustable, but for this work they are best set and left alone. For semi-arena or proscenium stage work, at least four 1,000-watt Fresnel spots are needed. Two on each side are the minimum requirement, with another four 500-watt spots to act as cyclorama or sidelights to cut the shadows which front lighting will always throw up.

Fresnel spots can be fitted with rotatable barn doors if a more direct beam with sharp cut-off is required. These lights should always be used with coloured celluloids. If there is no experienced advice available it is probably better not to think about lighting at all, but it is an interesting aspect of drama and a very professional subject in its own right.

The setting of a piece of work for presentation to an audience can add to its effectiveness, but simplicity can be just as effective as elaborate scenery and furniture. Try to avoid scene changes which require any sort of break in the continuity and certainly avoid cutting up the story by using front curtains. Arena presentations will involve the use of different levels and rostra which serve as seating, with possibly a door frame or archway if you need to indicate a character coming in from outside. Drama is always illusion and it is a source of constant surprise and delight that audiences will accept conventions. For instance, if a character has to enter a room and the only piece of scenery is a frame of the door, the audience will happily accept that they cannot see the character entering until a mime indicates that the door has been opened. Play on this acceptance of your convention and the onlookers become even more absorbed in the work.

In one or two of the playlets, a minimum of 'scenery' is indicated. For instance, in *Water, water, everywhere*, the ark is at first hidden behind a screen which is designed to fool some of the players into thinking that this is part of the garden. This screen need not cover the entire back of the stage. A small token screen with flowers painted on it will suffice and so long as the actors indicate that they cannot see what is beyond it, the audience will accept that they cannot see what is going on behind. If, however, the actors indicate that the audience can see what happens behind the screen but that some of the actors cannot, again, the audience will accept that convention. Truly, drama contains many elements of magic and deception.

Work presented on the proscenium stage or possibly semi-arena does give the opportunity to devise something of a set but, once again, simple suggestion is preferred to rigid reality.

For example, should the scene call for an archway entrance, it is better to suggest the arch with one pillar and the beginnings of a curve above, rather than to build a complete arch. It is cheaper, easier and more effective. Entrances are made easy since there is more space, and should a performer have to carry a banner or such like, he does not have the problem of dipping it as he comes through the arch. These are the sort of problems that lead to catastrophe.

Another scheme for easy entrance from the back of the stage is to suggest the scene on a backcloth of strips, rather like the plastic screens hung in open doorways in summer time. They obstruct the view but can be walked through with ease. Actors have no problems such as are set by opening and shutting doors.

In designing any set, colour is supremely important. With

a screen, a semi-archway, some rostra and a chair, using an effective colour scheme, lit by coloured celluloids from the four spotlamps above, any school can have a set comparable with those at Stratford Memorial Theatre. Teachers concerned with any kind of drama should go to see good professional productions and gather ideas which are effective and economic.

Speech

For the younger element in the age group we are considering, much of the work will be in the form of mime or dance and much less will be presented in the form of playlets. However at some time in a pupil's experience of drama, voice must enter into the work and this will need practice and experience. Elocution seems nowadays to be considered old-fashioned and all too often slovenly speech is accepted and possibly encouraged, especially when it is considered that the player should be 'natural'. This is very different from saying that the player should appear to be natural or homely or even slovenly. In all these circumstances good speech training is a requirement and I would suggest that teachers insist on this, even if it is only so that onlookers know what is going on.

Teachers need a basic knowledge of the techniques of speech and may find it helpful to study a textbook such as *Sound and Sense* by Wilton Cole. Material for use with young children can be found in books like *Puffin Book of Verse*, *Come Hither* by Walter de la Mare, and other anthologies. Pupils in the upper reaches of the middle school age range will find material in poems, short stories and extracts from favourite novels.

For instance, material for a short recital of Christmas items can be built up as follows:

(a) Dramatised reading from first section of *A Christmas Carol* by Charles Dickens. If this is suitably cut there is material for a Narrator, Scrooge, Nephew and Bob Cratchet.

(b) Excerpt from chapter *Winter and Summer* from *Cider with Rosie* by Laurie Lee, about the carol singers.

(c) Excerpt from chapter 'Dulce Domum' from *Wind in the Willows* by Kenneth Grahame, about the field mice as carol singers.

(d) *Ballad of the Bread Man* by Charles Causley.

(e) *Journey of the Magi* by T. S. Eliot.

Some of these may not be suitable but this is a suggestion for the kind of activity, and not only at Christmas time, that will encourage careful and effective speed. The series of books in *Junior Voices* and *Voices* contains a great store of material.

This is not the proper place to be too technical, but even so young students want to learn and it is well for the teacher to be aware of such techniques as pause, emphasis, colour, rate, modulation and so on.

So far as students are concerned, the techniques can be learnt and practised by using simple devices. Tongue twisters will help those who have difficulties with particular consonants. Inflexion can be improved by setting the student an exercise in which he has to carry on a telephone conversation using only one word or phrase, such as 'Yes', or 'I think so' or 'Really' and so on.

Use choral speech from time to time and let this build up into presented items with movement and mime accompanying the delivery of a poem by single voice or chorus. *The Daniel Jazz* in this book is set out as an example of this and there are many more such poems. Do not underestimate the ability of young people. One is constantly surprised by their ability if they are presented with appropriate material.

When presenting playlets it is vitally important that players know their words confidently, for only then will the meaning of the words get over to the audience.

Most schools now have recording equipment and one hopes this is used in speech development. A student will be more concerned over errors he hears for himself than over errors pointed out by others. Recording equipment can be used effectively in presentation. I have presented parts of Dorothy Sayers' *Man Born to be King* in tableaux accompanied by tape recordings of the script, very effectively. Previous recording of such work enables crowd discipline to be enforced more effectively.

In all this work be inventive and original and discuss all aspects with the performers. Whatever their age, they will have important ideas to contribute.

Improvisation

Work in Drama is essentially group work no matter what age group is being considered, and in Improvisation this is particularly true. This is not to say that individual improvisation is impossible, for then the audience becomes an essential part of the grouping, but for the purpose of this book, group improvisation is what we are concerned with. There are no age limits to groups working on Improvisation but the work does involve techniques of movement and mime so that in what is described here it is more appropriate to consider the students at the upper end of middle school grouping, that is to say those of twelve to thirteen years old.

Groups can be formed from any number of players, but something between twelve and eighteen is most convenient, allowing opportunity for considerable variety between emphasis on one or two players, two or three sub-groups, or total group participation.

Once the group is established the only other essential need is space, and that is space convenient for up to eighteen players to work in. It is possible to have too much space where the easy contact between players is lost, although the space should not be so small that work is cramped. Additional 'luxury' items are stage blocks to provide different levels and some form of apparatus to reproduce music and sound effects, a cassette player being the obvious, convenient method. Clothes should be light and easy to move in, props must be simple, and lighting a refinement that can be dispensed with until a group decides that its work is 'presentable' to an audience. With less experienced young players it is advisable to work initially on themes which are familiar and simple, concentrating on ideas that give opportunity for individuals to get used to working with a few colleagues and later being absorbed into the whole group.

Because Drama is concerned with living, there are really no bounds to what can be tackled but for our purposes we are considering Religious Education in its broadest sense, looking for opportunities to explore our relationship with others and the quality of spiritual experience.

The teacher may have to be something of a director at first but as the group becomes more experienced, ideas will come from the students, and the teacher should encourage these and use them as far as possible, for if ideas come from members of the group, these will be the important ones for them rather than those given by the teacher. Some students once asked their teacher, when looking for subjects, 'What shall we take?' His reply was, 'You have all the world to choose from.'

Improvisations can be mimed in silence, or played with dialogue or mimed to words spoken by a class, or played to appropriate background sound or music.

Make the first attempt simple, say 'People meeting'. The group imagine that they have been invited to a party. They are all going alone. Appoint two players as host and hostess. The players then enter one by one, are greeted and each offered a cup of coffee. As the group at the party increases, by mime each player demonstrates which of the company they get on well with, those who they do not like much and so on. Make the exercise fairly brief and if the group prefer allow words to be used.

Discuss this work, how do people in polite society show their feelings of liking and disliking, how did the players feel, and so on. Play the scene again, this time nominating the one or two who are generally unpopular and indicate beforehand a little clique who get on very well. Again, do not let the work drag on. Make it brief but follow with discussion. Do we sometimes practise social hypocrisy?

The group may then consider other situations where people meet. At a political meeting, at a meeting protesting against the construction of a new motorway, at church functions and so on. Allow speech at these but in general do not let such early work dry up.

Another starting point with the age group we are considering could be through a simple mimed story like *The Prodigal Son* or *Spit Nolan* in this book.

Poems are often useful starting points for improvisation,

particularly those that are important to young children; poems such as *The Snare* by James Stephens. This is about cruelty to animals and is certain to set off discussion. Some of the group will recite the poem. In verse speaking be imaginative in the distribution of verses and lines among the voices. When the verse speakers are well rehearsed, add improvised movement of animals, searchers, release from the snare at the end. Young children will feel the agony of this poem very clearly. From this starting point a number of improvisations can arise concerning all forms of cruelty to animals and men, with a lead into discussion of these issues.

Another James Stephens' poem, *The Cage*, can be dealt with in a similar way. When the group is more experienced, these two poems together with extracts from newspaper reports of local hunts, fishing competitions, some quotes from pamphlets put out by societies concerned with animal welfare, could be strung together with appropriate mime and action to make a 'programme', with added sound effects or music. All elements of Drama contribute to improvisation: speech, verse, mime, dance, characterisation, excerpts from plays, poems, magazine articles, and so on.

I would suggest that teachers read published texts such as *Improvisation* by Hodgson and Richards, and *Teaching Mime* by Rose Bruford.

The last three items among those suggested in this book are improvisations which can be attempted by the oldest students in our age range. They are difficult and could not be attempted by groups with little or no experience. Nevertheless they afford an opportunity to explore religious and spiritual concepts in a way that discussion alone does not encourage. They are set out as examples of the kind of dramatic experience which colour and heighten the religious development of young people.

The Seasons

A Dance-Mime

The appreciation of life-cycle comes slowly to young children and the preparation of this piece of work will afford opportunity to discuss the rhythm of the natural year through Winter, Spring, Summer, Autumn and round again to Winter. The constant recurrence of new life in Spring time can be emphasised and the religious faith which accepts that death is not final can be introduced and talked about. Obviously things in nature die, as we all do in due course, but observation of natural things can be an introduction to the concept that some element of each human life lives on. Discussion about spiritual life can develop from this.

This is merely an outline with suggestions arising from my own experience of working with young people from six to nine years old. Inevitably every piece of work will be unique, bearing the style of the teacher and the group doing the work. Allow a good deal of discussion and experimentation before finalising the form of the mime and even after that there will be room for spontaneity and improvisation.

The group should be split up into four sub-groups each representing one of the four seasons of the year: Spring, Summer, Autumn, Winter. In the dance the groups process around the arena, each in turn dominating the action but bringing the other groups into, and responding to, the action.

At some place in the circle around the arena there should be a focal point, say a small rostrum, sufficient for three or four players to form a significant group or tableau. Each group should have a banner bearer, the banner designed to indicate which season is being presented. There is scope here for relevant art work in the design and colouring of a banner to represent each season. As each 'season' is demonstrated, and as the focal point moves on, so the group moves round and the next successive banner moves on to the rostrum with a suitable tableau formed round it. The design of the banner, the dress of the members of the tableau, their attitudes and movement, all indicate which of the seasons is being presented.

The dance-mime begins with 'Spring'. With suitable music, poems, songs and movement, the theme of awakening, new life and growth is presented.

Spring

Dance-Mime	Select from the following and add your own ideas:
	Growth: Signs of new life and growth from the ground.
	The awakening of the Sun.
	April showers.
	Small animals: Puppies, kittens, ponies.
	Opening of flower buds.
Music	*l'Après-midi d'un faune* Debussy
	Selection from *Pastoral Symphony* Beethoven
	Slow movement—*Piano Concerto No. 21* Mozart
	Cavatina Myers
	'Spring' (*Four Seasons*) Vivaldi
Poems	Excerpt from *The Question* Shelley
	Green Rain Mary Webb
	The Spring John Lyly
	Ducks' Ditty Kenneth Grahame

The groups move round the arena, the banner and tableau representing Spring give place to 'Summer'. The group representing Summer takes over the arena from that representing Spring.

Summer

Dance-Mime	Holiday activities
	Sports and games
	The picnic – some amusement with wasps that won't go away; interfering animals, etc.

Fairground – roundabout, swings, coconut shy.

Suggest   For sports and games allow each member of the group to choose two games and mime one movement from each. For instance, leaping to save a goal at football and serving at tennis. Then, after practice, the actor puts the two actions together rhythmically. The combined movement can then be moved to music, creating a mini-ballet. This can later be extended to include three or four movements taken from summer games.

Music   Market Place: *Pictures at an Exhibition* Mussourgski

Market Place music: *My Fair Lady*   Fredk. Loewe

Cries of London   Traditional

Street Corner Overture   Rawthorne

London Symphony   Vaughan Williams

Rodeo   Copland

The groups move round to present Autumn. The predominant colour of the tableau costume can in this, as in other scenes, influence the mood of the season presented.

Autumn

Dance-Mime   Falling Leaves

Gathering the harvest

Harvest Home

Animals storing food for the winter

Music   Hymn: 'We plough the fields'

'See the farmer sow the seed'

'Autumn' (*Four Seasons*)   Vivaldi

Pavane for Dead Infanta   Ravel

Sea interludes from *Peter Grimes* Britten

Poems   *Beech Leaves*   James Reeves

The Wind   Christina Rosetti

The groups move round to present Winter.

Winter

Dance-Mime	Fading and dying
	Falling snow
	Snow men and snow fights
	Storms
	Hints of carols and Christmas
Music	*Requiem* Faure
	Cold Winter Sibelius
	Romeo and Juliet Tchaikovsky
	Shepherd Song Berlioz
Poems	*Fall leaves, fall* Emily Brontë
	For Snow Eleanor Farjeon
	Sleep Secure Sir Thomas Browne
	The Months Sara Coleridge

It is important that this section ends with stillness, a sense of finality, emphasised by music and, if available, lighting.

Then break in with joyful music and song, while the Winter scene gives way once more to Spring. The work ends with Spring dominating the scene and everyone moving, and possibly singing of new life. 'Who will buy this wonderful morning' from *Oliver* is the kind of song to suit this mood.

The work can be followed up with discussion of things dying and coming to life again. If the older pupils in the school could prepare and perform the 'St Joan' dance-mime, another lead would be given to the idea that a life does not just end with death. Without being precise, this sort of activity can help very young people to accept the cycle of life from youth to age to dying. This may well be of value to them should they encounter a death of a near-relative or friend when they are quite young.

The Good Samaritan

Mime-Narration

Probably the best way of describing this activity is to recount what happened when I decided to present it to a group of teachers attending a religious drama course. At the concluding session I included this mime, using a class of about thirty-five top Junior (ten- to eleven-year-old) boys and girls. The class teacher allowed me to work with them for four 30-minute sessions before they actually performed the mime in front of the teacher group.

During the first session, between us we made sure that we all knew the story and I described the style in which we were to present it. The teacher audience, representing a junior school at assembly, would sit all round the hall leaving us an area in the centre. The story was then analysed into scenes with the following scenario:

1 Departure from home.
2 The start of the journey – bidding friends goodbye.
3 The open country – a little rest.
4 The attack by bandits.
5 Left for dead.
6 The first traveller.
7 The second traveller.
8 The Samaritan.
9 The shelter of the inn.

During the second session we worked on the detail of each scene and casting. For instance, there was discussion about the traveller's house, his wife, his children, his dog and, would you believe it, the maid. I must have shown some hesitation about the maid until the young girl who had suggested this floored me by saying, 'If he was worth robbing he must have been rich and so probably had a maid.'

At this point I introduced the method of presentation which was mime to a musical accompaniment. I cut short some discussion which I might have allowed to develop over suitable music by limiting the choice and playing short excerpts.

We took 'Market Place' from *Pictures at an Exhibition* for the departure. It allowed hurried movement, signifying the bustle within a family when someone is setting off on a journey. The characters, traveller, wife, maid, three children and dog, all mimed their respective parts of packing, helping on with a coat, getting in the way, being pushed out of the way, remembering something forgotten, until at last the man was off, waving goodbye, children running after him for a final hug and so on. The music then became quieter, suggesting a hot day, and the man moved along on his journey, taking a circular route, at first meeting and greeting a number of people, then fewer and fewer until he was obviously alone and settled down for a rest. The class decided on a selection of part of Brahms' *Academic Overture* for this and faded it out as the man went to sleep.

For the attack the boys and girls chose 'The Rumble' from *West Side Story* and I introduced the mime technique of fighting without actually touching. The menacing robbers were scattered all over the arena, some near, some far from the traveller. In mime, and suiting action to the music, they beat him with fists and sticks and feet, one of them actually snatching his bag, until they departed hurriedly leaving him for dead.

A short excerpt from a slow movement from a piano concerto allowed the man to come to his senses, and this gave place to a slow solemn march while the Levite finds the man and fails to help him. There was no way we could see to denote a Levite and so the children just made him another traveller, the point being that he did not help.

Among the music played was some of *Façade* suite by William Walton, and the children liked it. They particularly liked 'Popular Song' and one lad moved very humorously to it. Feeling the need for a little light relief, they decided to make this lad a modern parson, dog collar, *pince nez* spectacles and all. His circuit, reading a prayer book close to his spectacles, was naturally very funny, and the boy nearly tripped over the body of the traveller, looked surprised, turned to several parts of his prayer book for guidance and, finding none, he sadly left the traveller, doing nothing about it.

It may sound strange to have a humorous interlude at that part but the children wanted it and I did not find it out of place at all.

'Lara's Theme' from the film *Dr Zhivago* immediately dispelled the humour and the Samaritan brought great compassion into the movement, finding the traveller, supporting him, caring for him, putting on bandages and helping him to his feet.

The children dispensed with the donkey, feeling that this was impracticable and any attempt to make up an animal from two children would have been too much like a pantomime.

The mime ended with 'Market Place' again as the Samaritan and traveller reached the busy inn where lots of people were interested in what had happened and lots of hands were ready to welcome the wounded man. The mime concluded with the Samaritan paying for the traveller's keep and leaving quietly and anonymously.

This account may be helpful. It could never be duplicated for each group of children will produce a different mime, each bearing an individual mark.

We had one complete rehearsal and then presented it to the teacher course. Because we had not over-rehearsed its impact was fresh and quite moving. The children involved had talked a great deal about cruelty, greed, force, compassion, unselfishness. I found considerable satisfaction when one of the youngest of the children said, 'You know, the Samaritan was the one that you would least expect to help that man,' and I was able to make the point that whereas the lawyer asked 'Who is my neighbour?' Jesus turned the question into 'Whom can I be neighbour to?'

Roaring Camp

A Playlet inspired by a story by
Bret Harte

SCENE: Young child going to bed. It is Christmas Eve.

CHILD Mummy, can you tell me a Christmas story tonight?
A very special one as it's Christmas Eve.

MOTHER I'll tell you about the baby Jesus.

CHILD Oh no, not that. We had that in school on Monday.

MOTHER Well, what about St Nicholas?

CHILD You told me that yesterday.

MOTHER So I did. King Wenceslas then?

CHILD No. We did a play about that. I was the page.

MOTHER Well, I don't think I know any others. Oh, yes I
do – a cowboy one.

CHILD That doesn't sound like Christmas, but tuck me in
and I'll listen.

MOTHER There was once a rough, tough cowboy town called
'Roaring Camp'. It was the wildest town you have ever
heard about. The cowboys were always fighting and shouting and shooting one another. There was only one saloon
in the town and every night it was rowdy and noisy and
quite dangerous to be in.

*The cowboys come rushing in demanding drinks and cigars
from the man behind the bar. Their women folk sit at
tables looking very cross, scolding the men. Jake and Jessie
serve at the counter.*

1ST COWBOY Come on, Jake, set up the drinks. It's thirsty
work out there on the prairie. What are you having,
Jasper?

2ND COWBOY Hey, let me through – my partner's got a drink
for me.

3RD COWBOY You wait your turn. I was here first. Hey, stop
pushing or I'll let you have it.

2ND COWBOY You and about six others, I guess. Let me through.

3RD COWBOY You've asked for it matey. Take that. (*He aims a blow but hits the wrong man.*)

4TH COWBOY What did you do that for? Just you come outside.

Amid general hubbub the two men go out feeling for their guns. A shot is heard.

4TH COWBOY (*returning*) Hey – funeral director. There's a job waiting for you outside.

Cowboys chatter as drinks are served.

1ST WIFE I'm about fed up with this sort of carry on. I've a good mind to leave and stay with my ma over in Blue Gulch.

2ND WIFE Me too. I do nothing but clean up after fighting. These men are rude, rough and rotten. I'll come with you if you will go.

3RD WIFE That's a good idea, why don't we all go? Then the men might miss us and we could promise to come back only if they behave themselves.

1ST WIFE The town's a disgrace. Rubbish all over the streets, houses want painting and roads full of pot holes. You never know how long you're going to have a husband anyhow.

4TH WIFE Let's go then.

Wives exit while hubbub continues in the saloon. Wives re-enter in hats and coats, each carrying a little case.

1ST COWBOY Hey, where do you think you're going?

2ND WIFE We're leaving, that's what.

3RD WIFE And we don't come back until you learn some manners.

2ND COWBOY You can't leave us. Who's going to cook and clean for us?

1ST WIFE From now on you look after yourself. We're going.

Wives leave.

1ST COWBOY Well, if that don't beat all? Come on, Jake, set up another round of drinks.

4TH COWBOY Now, what about you, Jessie, are you going to leave?

JAKE (*bar keeper*) You won't go, will you, Jessie? I rely on you to keep the saloon going.

ALL No, Jessie – you can't leave.

JESSIE (*quietly*) It would serve you all right if I did go. You are a disgraceful crowd. You ill-treat your wives. You are ungracious and rude, sometimes downright cruel. You drink too much and you gamble too much. There isn't a house that isn't falling down from neglect and the streets are untidy and dangerous. As for the noise of shouts and gun shots – it's unbearable. I'm not surprised the women left. But I'm not going. You see, I'm going to have a baby.

A silence, while they take in this news.

JAKE Is this true, Jessie? How wonderful. Lads, I'm going to be a Dad. Let's all have a drink.

General shouts of 'Whoopee' etc.

1ST COWBOY Hey, quiet you lot. Shut up over there and listen to me. (*Noise subsides.*) If Jessie is going to have a baby, she'll need to do less work in the bar. Any volunteers to do an hour or so each day. Come on, any volunteers? (*No response.*)

1ST COWBOY (*drawing his gun*) I said – Any volunteers?

Several cowboys put up a hand to volunteer.

1ST COWBOY That's good. Now Jessie, you'll need a cradle for the baby. You, Stumpy Sam, get out your horse and buggy and go into Blue Gulch and fetch a soap box.

SAM What's a soap box? I've never heard of soap before.

He looks as if he hasn't!

2ND COWBOY Soap is what you wash with. You know – on your birthday. Go and get the box, and bring some soap with it. Jessie's room will need a clean up before the baby comes.

1ST COWBOY Say, while you're there, fetch some paint and paint brushes. We'll smarten up the inn. We can't have a baby growing up in a dirty place like this.

4TH COWBOY Yes, and the outside of our houses could do with a clean-up. Will you be good enough to bring some garden tools and some seeds so that we can grow flowers, Sam, please?

5TH COWBOY (*astonished*) Did you hear him say 'please'.

6TH COWBOY That's a word I ain't heard in a long time.

Sam goes.

1ST COWBOY Now, you go off and have a rest, Jessie. We'll look after the bar. And no noise from any of you while Jessie is having a rest.

JAKE And in case any of you'se fellows get bad ideas – I suggest you all put your guns in this box. There'll be no street fighting from now on.

Cowboys and wife form tableau.

CHILD I liked that story, Mummy, but it wasn't really a Christmas story.

MOTHER But it was. You see, Roaring Camp was a terrible place with quarrels and bad temper, but all that changed when the child was born. That child changed the characters of the people and Roaring Camp became a better place. The world was like that until Jesus was born. After that very first Christmas when the baby boy Jesus came into the world, the world has become a better place.

CHILD Oh yes, I see now. It really was a Christmas story.

Children sing 'The Cowboy Carol' (Cecil Broadhurst)

The Legend of Saint Nicholas

A Playlet for Christmas

This is a simple play which might well be performed at an assembly just before the Christmas holidays.

SCENE The Market Place. The people are busily buying things for Christmas.

TOY STALL KEEPER Come along, come along. Everything here for the children's Christmas. Dolls, toys and games. Here they are, everything you could want. Here's a fine toy sledge – strong enough to take two youngsters and no fear of breaking. Come along, who'll buy?

SARAH You know, Dick, we won't have any money for toys this year. It isn't your fault that you're out of work and have been for the past three months, but once I've bought a little extra food for Christmas Day, there'll be nothing to spare.

DICK I know that, Sarah. The children will have to make do with one or two toys I can make myself, but they won't be much good. I'm not very good at making toys. What did Mary say she wanted?

SARAH Well, Mary wants a doll's house and John says he wants a Noah's ark and some wooden animals.

DICK I'll have to see what I can do. Hello, Bertha, how's your husband, Tom, today?

BERTHA Not very well, I'm afraid. It's this cold weather. Really gets into his bones, it does. No matter how many blankets I heap on top of him, he can't get warm. I get out for a while in the morning to cut some wood for our fire, but it don't last long and then the house goes cold again. I do miss the wood that our Tom used to cut.

SARAH You must be having a hard time just now. There's so much illness about. I'm sorry for the very old folk too. There's an old couple just by us and both of them are poorly. They hardly get out at all and I know they are short of food. How they manage, I don't know.

DICK They could both do with milk, eggs and a few slices of good roast meat, but there's not much chance of that. They live on thin soup most of the time, made of precious little more than water and a handful of peas.

BERTHA Well, I can't stop talking here. I'll see if the baker is selling off a stale loaf or two and then I must be getting back. I'm aching all over from that wood cutting.

She goes out

SARAH Goodbye then – Happy Christmas. Have as good a time as you can and I do hope Tom is up and about soon.

DICK Come on then, Sarah, let's be getting home. By the way, did you see that fellow from the Big House over in the corner? He looks pretty well off – don't suppose he'll go hungry this Christmas. What do they call him? Nicholas, isn't it?

SARAH Yes, he's not long been up there – seems a nice sort. Come on, Dick.

They go out.

Nicholas comes down from where he has been standing and looks at some notes he has made on a piece of paper. He has a fine red coat and long boots. His little cap matches the coat.

NICHOLAS Well, I am sorry for those folks. They won't have much of a Christmas unless I do something about it. Let's see, what must I get. A doll's house, a Noah's ark, a large sack of wood, some milk, eggs and good roast meat. I'll see what I can do.

He goes out.

The scene shifts to the houses up the hill. Three doors open on to the stage (these need be no more than a frame or even a space between two chairs back to back). It is midnight. We hear the sound of approaching sleigh bells which stop just off stage.

Enter Nicholas with a parcel which could well hold a doll's house and a Noah's ark. He does look a bit like Father Christmas.

NICHOLAS (*to the reindeer off stage*) Whoa there! Steady on – keep the sleigh still. I won't be a minute. Now, which is the house of Sarah and Dick? Oh, there it is. I'll just put the sack with the doll's house and Noah's ark in it on their doorstep and they'll find them tomorrow morning.

He goes out and returns with another sack.

Now, here is a sack of chopped wood. I'll leave that outside Bertha's home. Now, I'll just get the other sack with the food in it and that will please the old couple when they get up tomorrow.

He goes out to return with a third sack.

Now that should be a nice surprise for them all – quite a good Christmas present, but I don't want them to know who has given them so off I'll go.

He goes out and we hear the jingle of the bells fading in the distance.

The lights fading and rising again indicate that it is morning.

DICK (*emerging lazily from his house*) Oh dear, I am tired. I wish you children hadn't kept me awake. (*To himself.*) What a pity they haven't got any real toys. Oh, well, it can't be helped. (*As he turns to go back into the house he sees the sack.*) Sarah! Kids! come here. Look what I've found on our doorstep. (*His wife and children come hurrying out.*)

BOY What is it, Dad? Where has this sack come from?

DICK I don't know – open it up anyhow.

GIRL See, there's a doll's house. It must be for me.

BOY And I've got a Noah's ark. It's great. And there's a box of cigars for you, and a box of chocolates for you, Mum.

SARAH What a surprise. I wonder who left them.

BOY It's a real surprise Christmas present. And there are sacks

BERTHA (*coming out from her house*) What's all the noise about? Who left this sack on my doorstep? Why, it's full of chopped wood. And a turkey on the top. We'll have a party tonight and it will make Tom really well. Wherever did all this come from?

OLD MAN (*coming from his house*) You are making a noise. I know it's Christmas, but we do want a bit of quiet. What's this sack doing on my doorstep?

BERTHA Someone has been doing a good turn. Look in the sack, see what he has left you.

OLD MAN Why, it's full of food. Eggs, milk, bread, and all sorts of things. It will be a good Christmas. I'll take them in to my wife.

He goes.

DICK Come on, kids, let's get all this inside.

They all leave except Sarah and Bertha.

SARAH I wonder who did all this. Did you see anything?

BERTHA Well, as a matter of fact I did. I think I saw a sledge pulled by reindeer come up the hill and stop here. Then a man in snow boots, a red coat with white fur and a little red hat, put all these gifts at the doors. Did you see anything?

SARAH I thought I saw that happen too. And the man in the coat looked very like Nicholas who lives at the Big House.

BERTHA I thought so too. You know, if he does this sort of thing for people he ought to be made a saint: Saint Nicholas, would you believe?

SARAH Yes, and it wouldn't be long before that got shortened to Santa Claus. Do we say anything about this to the others?

BERTHA No, let's keep it a secret. Some secrets are worth keeping, aren't they!

The Story of Prahlada

Mime-Narration

This is a story from the Hindus which is filled with the assumptions and spirit of the Hindu religion, while the speeches of Prahlada are convenient summaries of basic Hindu teaching.

This simple setting can provide an introduction to the study of the Hindu faith and practice, with opportunities to discuss similarities with other religious teaching. The playlet gives opportunity for a number of children to be involved and create a meaningful mime-narration within the framework of the story.

Scene: The court room of King Hiran. Courtiers are seen in small groups.

1ST COURTIER The King returns today from the battles. Wherever he has gone, he has been victorious over his enemies.

2ND COURTIER Yes, but always he wins by foul play and treachery. He is far from being a good man in spite of his victories over three worlds.

1ST COURTIER He calls himself God of riches, Judge of the dead, and mightier than all the great gods put together. That is wickedness.

3RD COURTIER I am sorry for his son, Prahlada, trained in vice and wickedness by his old teacher. He will grow up to be more cruel and wicked than his father.

4TH COURTIER (*announcing arrival of the King*) Bow low before your illustrious ruler, King of three worlds – your mighty King Hiran.

Enter the King and others. They act foolishly with shouts and laughing as if slightly intoxicated.

HIRAN Bring to me my son, Prahlada, and his tutor. Let me

see for myself that he is being trained to rule the people in my way.

Prahlada is escorted in with his tutor. Prahlada and his tutor bend low.

HIRAN Here now, get up and tell me what you have learned.

PRAHLADA In obedience to your command, I will recite. I have learned to love the great God who is without beginning or end, the Lord of Life and the World, the universal cause.

HIRAN (*angrily*) What! Who taught you that treachery. I am the great God! You, vile teacher, what is this nonsense you have taught him?

TUTOR Oh King, what your son has just uttered was not taught by me.

HIRAN Who then? Who taught you this lesson? Your teacher denied it was his teaching.

PRAHLADA The great god, Vishnu, father, he is the supreme teacher of all the world.

HIRAN Blockhead – who is this Vishnu who you say taught you?

PRAHLADA He is the supreme Lord from whom all things proceed. His glory cannot be described.

HIRAN Are you so keen to die that you give the title of Supreme Lord to anyone else while I live?

PRAHLADA Vishnu is the creator and protector of all, even you, Father. You should not be afraid or offended.

HIRAN Take this wretched boy away and let his teacher take from him the lying praise of my enemy, Vishnu.

Prahlada is led out by the tutor and a passage of time is indicated.

HIRAN Now, fetch my son once more. Perhaps the lies he was speaking when I saw him last have been trained out of him.

Prahlada is presented.

Now, my son, repeat what your teacher has now instilled into you.

PRAHLADA May he from whom matter and soul originate,
              From whom all that moves or is unconscious proceeds,

> He who is the cause of all this creation, Vishnu,
> Be favourable unto us.

HIRAN Kill the wretch. He is a traitor to me and all his friends.

Attendants beat Prahlada but he does not feel the blows. (This may be performed in a ritual mime to music with great effect, the attendants circling about Prahlada as they beat him, but are not actually within striking distance.) As they beat, Prahlada recites:

PRAHLADA As truly as Vishnu, who is everywhere, is present in your weapons and in my body, so truly shall these weapons fail to hurt me.

Hiran commands poisonous serpents to bite him to death. These attack him but he is unharmed and feels no pain for the boy meditates on Vishnu. Another opportunity for effective dance.

SNAKES We have broken our fangs but the boy is unhurt.

Hiran commands the elephants to attack him. This they do but he is unhurt.

ELEPHANTS Our tusks have been blunted and the boy remains unhurt.

HIRAN Send away the elephants and let fire consume him.

A great heap of wood is piled around the boy and the fire is lit. The boy remains unhurt. A fire dance can be performed here.

FLAMES We have been blown by the winds and have raged round the boy but he remains unhurt.

Brahmin priests enter.

PRIEST O King, cease to be angry with your son. Let us teach him. We will teach him all truth. We will teach him the lessons of sorrow, the need for the eternal, a love for all men and all creatures, the science of government for the good of all and through it all we will teach him great songs of praise.

Prahlada is escorted away by the priests.

The Servant Girl's Brooch

A Playlet which emphasises that everyone
is important, however humble their contribution.

NARRATOR This little incident takes place in a far distant land where the people loved to make images and statues of the God they worshipped.

Enter the King and his court.

KING Bring in the High Priests of the great temple, for I have a new order to give them.

COURTIER Enter and stand before the King.

The High Priests come in.

KING Listen to me. We have many pictures and images and statues of our God and most of them are very beautiful. However, I want a new statue made that will be more beautiful than anything I have ever seen. See to it that this magnificent statue will be ready within three months.

CHIEF PRIEST But, Your Majesty, we have very little money left to build statues. We have spent all but the last few pence on the set of paintings you ordered for the entrance to the temple. What little money we have left will be needed for the upkeep of the buildings. We could not possibly have the new statue ready within three months.

KING I had no idea that the Royal Treasury was so low. Steward, what have you to say to this? How can we possibly create this beautiful statue that I have set my heart on?

STEWARD There is only one way, Your Majesty, and that is to ask all your loyal subjects to donate money and gifts towards a fund that will provide enough to create your beautiful statue. There are many wealthy people who will willingly subscribe.

CHIEF PRIEST That is so, Your Majesty, and we can send out our priests to all parts of the country and collect large and small amounts, which together will make great sums of money. Where precious metals are donated, these can be melted down and included in the great work.

KING So be it. I will leave the arrangements to you and my stewards. Report to me when I can view the beautiful statue.

The King and court depart. The Steward and Priests confer.

STEWARD I will draw up lists of the many regions in the kingdom and the priests can go out into the country, each receiving gifts from different parts. *Steward departs.*

CHIEF PRIEST Good. You, priests, will then travel with horses and baskets collecting money and gifts. Remember that the King wants a magnificent statue and you must persuade the people to give up some of their precious objects.

PRIEST Can we collect from the poorer people? Are they allowed to make contributions?

CHIEF PRIEST You must use your discretion. Remember, above all, that the statue must be beautiful.

Steward returns.

STEWARD Here are the lists of our people in all the regions of the kingdom. Set out at once and return with all the gifts as soon as possible. We will set up a curtain, here in this room, and the space will be kept for our craftsmen to work. All the precious metals will be melted down and cast in the mould of the statue. When all is finished, the King will come to see the unveiling of the statue. Here are the regional lists. Get to work as soon as you can.

He distributes the lists and all disperse.

NARRATOR We now travel to the house of a wealthy merchant who employs many servants in his household.

Enter merchant, his wife, her servant girl, and men with boxes

MERCHANT Bring in that big box. Take care; it is full of very costly ornaments and jewellery. The collectors from the

King are coming today to gather in our contributions towards the great statue of our God.

MERCHANT'S WIFE I am sorry to lose so much of my jewellery, but I am sure it is good to give it in order to make beautiful things that people for years to come will see. Have you brought my special jewel box, Esther?

ESTHER (*the servant girl*) Yes, madam, and I think you have been very generous to give so much. Here come the priests.

PRIEST (*entering*) Sir, we are all very grateful to you for giving so much. The new statue will honour our God and bring joy to us and our descendants. Thank you, indeed. Now, men, will you bring your gifts down to the road where I have a cart waiting. Take care now! Off you go. Good day to you.

All leave except Priest and servant girl

ESTHER Sir, I have no valuable jewellery, nor have I money to give, but I have this pretty brooch which my mother gave me. Will you take that as a contribution towards the great statue?

PRIEST Well, thank you, my dear. It is a very nice little brooch. It is kind of you to give it.

ESTHER Thank you, sir. (*She goes.*)

PRIEST (*looking at brooch*) This is a cheap little thing. I can't imagine this mixing with all the gold and silver that we already have. It would spoil the good metal if this were melted down with it. I will put it in my pocket. The girl will never know that her gift was not included.

NARRATOR The great collection was made and then the goldsmiths and silversmiths melted down all the precious metals and a cast of the statue was built. Nobody saw the work for it was carried out behind the screen as the King had ordered. The great day arrived on which the clay mould was to be broken open. The King was one of the first to see the statue.

The crowd enters and makes way for Chief Priest, King and court. The King stands before the screen or curtain.

CHIEF PRIEST Your Majesty, the cast around the statue is now to be broken open. When this is done the screen will be removed and you will be the first to see the magnificent statue.

There is a sound of the clay cast being broken and the curtain or screen is removed. The statue we now see is hideous.

KING What is this? I wanted a beautiful statue and this is horrible. The colours have all run into each other, the precious stones are badly set and the face is ugly. Melt the metals down and remake the statue.

NARRATOR (*as tableau freezes*) Four times the craftsmen melted the metal down and four times the result of their work was hideous.

KING This is the fourth time I have come here to see the result of your work and each time you show me this ugly result. Draw the curtain so that I don't have to look at it. Now, why is this happening? Do you have any suggestions, Chief Priest?

CHIEF PRIEST I am at a loss to explain it. I am sure that everything that was used to make the statue was good. It should have made a beautiful statue.

QUEEN You say that everything you put in was good, but did you leave anything out?

CHIEF PRIEST No, I used all the wonderful gifts that we received. I don't think anything was left out, was it?

PRIEST (*coming forward*) Well, as a matter of fact, I have a small gift in my pocket. It was given by a young servant girl in a rich man's household. I didn't think it was good enough. Here it is, a very cheap brooch made of poor metal with a blue glass for a stone.

QUEEN Maybe that is just what is missing. Tell the craftsmen to try once more and this time use the servant girl's brooch.

NARRATOR Once more the craftsmen set to work, this time including the servant girl's brooch. When the work was done, once again the King and his court stood before the screen waiting for the statue to be unveiled.

KING Now, once more, let us have the cast broken open so that we can see this statue.

There is a sound of the workmen breaking open the clay cast – the curtain or screen comes open and we see a fine statue with the blue stone of the girl's brooch set in the centre of the forehead. There are gasps of joy and words of appreciation.

CHIEF PRIEST There, sir, now we have indeed got a worthy statue.

KING Yes, indeed, it will be a source of joy to all of us. Let us learn a lesson from this experience. To achieve anything in the community that is good, we cannot afford to neglect even the poorest contribution. It could well be that that tiny and humble effort is just what is needed to achieve the greatest success.

The Story of Ruth

Mime-Narration

This is a difficult but effective piece of work. The players have to react to the story in the narration, yet in their mime convey their feeling for what is probably the loveliest story in the Bible. It is a story of Faith, Loyalty and Love, and for that reason alone is worth attempting. The players must know the story well and must have discussed at length the relationships existing between the characters. The story needs to be narrated since miming alone will probably leave the audience unaware of what is going on.

The narration can accompany the mime or the piece may be played with alternate narration and mime. If the group is not experienced in mime, it may be preferable to present a tableau to accompany each section of the narrative. The narration can be split up and shared between a number of speakers and some sections may well be spoken by small choral groups. There is scope for a good deal of discussion and inclusion of original ideas. This is an appropriate piece of work for Harvest time since in the Jewish religion the story of Ruth was always told at the festival of Shovuos, the celebration of the gathering of the barley harvest.

Commentary

More than a thousand years before Jesus was born there lived a Jewish family in Bethlehem. Naomi was the wife of Elimelech and they had two sons who worked in the fields with their father.

They were a happy, hard-working family until famine came to the country and the ground would yield no crops. Elimelech told his wife and sons that they must pack up and go to another country where there was no famine.

They travelled north until they reached the river Jordan and having crossed this, they moved south again until they reached Moab, a country to the west of the Dead Sea.

They were happy there until Elimelech, the husband of Naomi, died.

However, soon after that both the boys married Moabite girls, Orpah and Ruth. You must remember that the girls were not Jewish and had their own, different religion. The family was happy together for nearly ten years.

Sadly, then, both the boys died and the three unhappy women were left alone. Naomi knew that she must now go back to her own birthplace, Bethlehem.

She tried to persuade the two girls not to come with her since they knew nothing of Israel and would be regarded as foreigners.

However, they both insisted on going with her and the three women set off on the return journey and reached the river Jordan once more.

Here, Orpah decided to go back and Naomi tried to persuade Ruth that she did not have to go any further. But Ruth had made up her mind and declared that she would spend the rest of her life with her husband's mother. She said:

> 'Wherever you go, I will go.
> Wherever you live, I will live.
> Your people shall be my people,
> And your God, my God.
> Wherever you die, I will die,
> And there I will be buried.'

Seeing that she was determined to go with her, Naomi said no more.

When the two women reached Bethlehem, they saw the people in the fields taking in the harvest.

Boaz was the wealthy owner of the land and he allowed poor people to walk behind the reapers and pick up any corn that was left on the ground. This was called gleaning.

Boaz saw Ruth and was attracted to her. He told his farm workers to see that plenty of corn was left for her to glean and he also told them to give her water whenever she wanted it.

When Ruth went home she told Naomi about Boaz and learnt from Naomi that he was a distant relative of hers and according to Jewish law had some responsibility for Naomi and for her relatives.

At night the workers slept on the floor of the threshing room and that night Ruth made a point of sitting at the feet of Boaz so that he saw her when he awoke. They were in love with each other and Boaz sought to marry her.

But there was a nearer relative to Naomi who had prior claim to Ruth. However, he gave up his claim and showed this in the traditional way, by taking off his shoe and offering it to Boaz, before witnesses.

Boaz married Ruth and there was a great, festive marriage feast.

In due course Ruth had a son named Obed, who had a son called Jesse: who had a son called David who became one of the most famous of the kings of Israel.

A thousand years later, a descendant of David, named Joseph, had to travel with his wife, Mary, back to the family town, Bethlehem, to be counted in a census. While he was there, Mary gave birth to a son, whom they called 'Jesus'.

Water, Water Everywhere

A Playlet about the Flood

This little play could be given on a special occasion by a group performing for the school, or as a presentation to parents at end of term or some such event. This must be played in semi-arena form or on a raised area in front of the audience because it is necessary for the players to go behind a painted canvas where they cannot be seen. The canvas is painted to represent a garden while behind it is something to represent the ark. It must be possible to roll up or move this canvas easily. The ark need be no more elaborate than stage blocks arranged at different levels with some representation of bow and stern.

The first part should be presented rather for fun, light-heartedly, but when Noah comes to the explanation of the rainbow as God's promise or covenant, the scene should take on a more serious tone. Do not be tempted to give Noah a beard in order to make him look old. Let his age show in the acting.

PLAYERS

NOAH Philosophic, obedient to God's will but just a little bit tetchy.

MRS NOAH Rather bossy but irritated when she finds she cannot rule Noah.

SHEM Practical but far sighted.

HAM Lazy – likes to have a good time.

JAPHETH Dreamy and spiritual.

EVA (*Shem's wife*) Adores her husband.

SARAH (*Ham's wife*) Practical, wants to get things done.

NAOMI (*Japheth's wife*) Very like her husband, a visionary.

PLAYLET

NOAH (*appearing from behind the screen with a mallet in his hand. He looks up into the sky.*) I've started the job you gave me, Lord. I can't think why you told me to build such a big boat. After all, there are only eight of us and the boat's big enough to carry everyone in the village with lots of room to spare. (*He pauses, as though listening to someone.*) You say we shall have some visitors! Some animals? What sort of animals? Nothing dangerous I hope. Oh! all sorts of animals. Two of each, you say. Elephants as well. Oh dear, no wonder we shall need a big boat.

Enter Shem.

Oh, Shem, I'm glad you've come along. I want you to give a hand with a job I'm doing.

SHEM Sorry, Dad, I'm busy. The old lady who keeps the shop on the corner wants some shelves fixed. I must hurry.

NOAH You'll have to leave that. My work is much more important and there are one or two things I can't manage on my own.

SHEM Why, whatever are you up to? How do you think I can help?

NOAH (*secretly*) Well, nobody knows about this, but I'm – er – building a boat.

SHEM (*laughing*) What do you mean, building a boat. There's no water within miles from here where you could sail it. Anyway, you don't know anything about sailing.

NOAH Well, it isn't exactly a sailing boat – it's a sort of floating boat.

Enter Ham and Japheth.

SHEM I say you two – guess what Dad's up to? He's building a boat.

HAM Whatever for – there's no lake nearer than ten miles and that dries up for six months of the year. What sort of boat have you got in mind, Dad? We'd better put wheels on it. (*They all laugh.*)

JAPHETH Look here, stop laughing at Dad. Can't you see he's serious about it. Whatever gave you this idea, Dad?

Noah sits on a box or bench while the boys sit around him.

NOAH Well, I had a dream and in the dream I was told by God that because the people in His world were so wicked, cheating each other, stealing from each other, not working hard and only thinking of themselves, He was going to start all over again by causing such heavy rains to fall that the whole world would be flooded and all creatures destroyed. But to start things up again one family must survive, together with a male and female of every kind of creature, animal and bird. Now, the amazing part of this story is that He has chosen our family to be saved and it will be for us to start the world off again when the flood waters go down. For us, and all the creatures, to live through the flood we need a great boat and that's what I'm building.

SHEM You're pulling our legs, surely. Why should God choose us? We're not very special.

HAM Well, I think it's all nonsense. You've been dreaming all right, Dad, and it's time you woke up.

JAPHETH I'm not so sure. Perhaps there is going to be a great flood. Certainly the world is wicked and it would not be surprising if God were angry with the people in the world. Where is the boat, Dad?

NOAH (*getting up*) Well, take a look at this part of the garden. Try to pick some of the flowers.

The boys discover that the canvas is a painted garden.

HAM They're not real – they're painted on canvas.

NOAH That's my secret. Now, pull on that rope and roll up the canvas. (*They do so*) There's my boat.

SHEM Why, it's enormous! Why is it so big?

NOAH Well, you see, we have got to take two of every kind of animal. When we come out of the ark after the flood the animals can have pups and kittens and calves and all sorts of baby animals to start the world off again.

JAPHETH Dad did have the dream. He really did have a message from God. We must all help.

SHEM Yes, come on, you two. Get the canvas screen down again and we'll help Dad get the boat finished.

They lower the screen.

HAM We'd better not tell our wives until the last minute. Then it won't be quite such a shock.

NOAH Good boys. Let's get to work and finish the job before the rains come.

They go behind the screen and we hear hammering and sawing from time to time.
Mrs Noah and the wives come in.

MRS NOAH Wherever have those men got to? They're never here when they are wanted. I wanted Noah to fix up a sunshade on the roof. This weather is stifling hot and it's impossible to stay indoors without feeling baked.

EVA But it's nice and cool in the shade of the garden. I've never seen the flowers looking so colourful. We seem to have quite a number of plants and flowers I've never seen before.

NAOMI Some of the flowers are taller than they were last year. You know, that used to be a dusty piece of land and now it's covered with very pretty flowers.

Sound of men working.

SARAH Whatever is all that noise? It sounds like hammering and sawing and it's coming from behind that garden.

MRS NOAH The men are up to something. It's funny that the flowers have grown there. I didn't plant any in that place. Why, they are not flowers at all. They are pictures of flowers painted on canvas. Noah! Noah! Where are you? What are you up to? What's all the noise about?

Noah and the boys appear from behind the screen.

NOAH Now don't carry on, Ma. I can explain everything.

SARAH Look at your coat, Ham. You've got sawdust all over it.

MRS NOAH What's going on, I'd like to know? What have you got behind that screen?

SHEM All right, I'll explain. Dad had a dream and in it God told him that for its wickedness the world was to be destroyed by flood. Dad was told to build a great boat so that one family, ours! could be saved, together with two of every kind of animal, to start the world all over again when the flood went down.

They all stand silent and wondering while the screen is raised.

NAOMI I feel that this is true. The world is wicked and we are highly honoured by God to be the ones to start a new life in a new world. See, the sky is already becoming darker. Let us prepare for our stay in the ark.

EVA Look, the animals are moving to us. Let us get on board and prepare for the journey.

The family and animals board the ark to appropriate music. There is the sound of rain falling and the storm begins. For storm music see suggestions in list at end of the book. The players mime the movement of the boat.

NOAH See, the clouds are passing but the flood waters are as high as ever. How can we know when it is safe to leave our refuge?

SARAH Why can't we release one of the birds? It will fly around and if there is no land to rest on it will come back.

SHEM What a good idea. If it doesn't come back we will know that the waters have gone down and we shall soon be able to leave the ark.

NOAH I will do that. Bring one of the ravens to me.

Noah mimes the release of the raven. They all watch it into the distance while the flight of the raven is accompanied by music recorded or played.

MRS NOAH Well, it hasn't come back. But I can't see that the water has gone down at all. We can't go out of the ark in this.

NAOMI Father, send out a dove, the bird of peace, to see whether God is no longer angry with His people.

NOAH Yes, I'll do that.

Noah mimes the release of the dove, which flies away and then returns.

HAM Oh, dear, we shall have to stay cooped up in this old boat for ages. Have another try, Dad. Send the dove out again.

Noah sends out the dove which returns with an olive twig.

SHEM It's an olive branch in its beak. We shall always remember the olive branch as a sign of peace and goodwill.

MRS NOAH It won't be long before we leave the boat. Get ready to unload.

NAOMI Send out the dove once more so that we can be sure of God's good will.

Noah mimes the release of the bird, which does not return.

NOAH The dove does not return. It has found its home and now we are settled once more on dry land.

NAOMI See, a coloured bow has stretched across the sky. It is a rainbow. What can it mean?

NOAH It tells of God's promise to us and to all living creatures that never again will such a terrible thing happen between God and man. We must keep our part of the bargain to try to use God's gifts only for the good of all, and God for His part will make crops to grow for our food and provide all we need for our life here on earth. Let us leave the ark. Let us build an altar to God and give thanks for our safety.

The family build an altar and kneel around it as the animals move out from the ark.

The Prodigal Son

Mime-Narration

This story is told by a commentary to mimed scenes. The mime gives opportunity for a number of children to take part, and the speaking of the narrative can be shared by any number of children. This work can be performed by the younger children in the age range with which we are concerned. Mime is probably easier than tableaux, although presentation by means of a series of tableaux would also be effective. Musical backing can be added to enhance the movement in some of the scenes and this will also heighten the varying moods of the story. There is a list of titles that have been found useful at the end of this book.

Commentary

One of the stories Jesus told to the people who followed him was about forgiveness and concerns two brothers who helped their father to run his farm. With all the other workers, both the boys helped in sowing the seed, reaping the harvest, binding the corn and storing the grain in sacks until it was sold in the markets. The farm was a very busy and prosperous binding the corn and storing the grain in sacks until it was sold in the markets. The farm was a very busy and prosperous one.

The father of the two boys was sad to see that his younger son did not enjoy the work and that he lost interest, and indeed grew quite lazy. One day when he saw him idling his time away the father asked him what he wanted to do. The boy said he would like to travel and asked his father to give him the share of the farm that would be his eventually.

The father agreed and handed over a lot of money so that the boy could make his own way in life. However, the father warned his younger son that when he, the father died, all that was left of the farm would belong to the older boy. The young son agreed and said his 'Goodbyes' to his father, his brother and all the farm workers.

The young boy set out and soon found friends who drank with him, and ate with him, and came to his parties. It was the young boy who paid for everything and he did not find any difficulty in making more and more friends.

But his money did not last for ever. There came a time when he could no longer pull a bundle of notes from his pocket and, when this happened, his new friends quickly left him and he found himself poor and alone.

Now, when his new-found friends came by, he would ask them to help him, but they soon brushed him aside and, as he got poorer and poorer, they passed by without a glance.

The young boy begged for work on the farms but nobody would employ him, until one farmer said he wanted a pig-man. The farmer took the boy to the pigs and told him to make up their meal out of scraps of food thrown out from the kitchen and clean out the pig-stye. When the boy asked what he would get to eat, the farmer said he must eat with the pigs. And what is more, he had to find a place to sleep at night, inside the pig-stye.

The young boy was terribly sad and wondered whatever he could do. He fed the pigs, he cleaned out the stye, he even brought himself to eat some of their food. He had never been so sad in his life. Whatever could he do?

Then he made up his mind. He would get up and go back to his father. He would say how sorry he was to have left home. He would ask for the meanest, poorest job on his father's farm. He would ask for the lowest of wages and the poorest of food. He did not deserve anything better, but he would like to be home once more.

At his father's farm, work was going on as usual, the older brother doing most of the work of managing the farm while the father could often be seen looking away down the road by which his other son had left. Every day he hoped the young boy would come back.

Then, he saw the young boy in the distance, dragging himself along to get home. The father picked up a cloak and ran down the road to meet his son. He put the cloak over his shoulder and brought the boy back gladly. The farm workers were pleased and gathered round to greet the prodigal.

The father gave orders for a great party to be prepared. Food was brought out, musicians played, and everybody had a good time. While this party was going on, the older brother, who had been working out in the fields, came home. He asked what was going on and when he was told that the father was giving a special party for his young brother who had come back, he felt very angry and would not go in.

As the older boy stood alone outside, the father came out to him. It was difficult to explain but the older brother understood that he had enjoyed the comfort of home and his father's company all the time, while the young boy, his own fault it is true, had suffered the sadness of being away, being alone, feeling that nobody cared. The older brother then realised that he was really the lucky one, and with his father went in to enjoy the party.

Genesis and Nativity

A Dance-Mime

The object of this piece of work is to explore a parallel between the Creation of the World and Rebirth through the Nativity of Jesus.

This is not the sort of work that can be attempted by young people with little experience of movement. Its impact depends on very good, expressive movement and considerable co-operation between the dancers. It can be an extremely moving and effective experience.

The work is accompanied by sound and music produced by percussion, recorders and selected recordings. Costume needs are not demanding and it is suggested that leotards and cloaks of varying texture and colour are all that are required. Masks and hats can be every effective.

The work should be preceded by a great deal of discussion about the theme and, to help the movement, on words like: dark, light, conflict, serenity, procession, soaring, circling, darting, swirling, extending, light, ponderous and so on. From this discussion will follow practice movement to words, sounds and music. Each style of movement will only look natural with practice. Simplicity, to be effective, demands planning, practice and discipline. Lighting can be an advantage, if it is available, but lack of professional equipment need not deter from attempting this sort of presentation. No set is required and the most effective performance is probably in an arena with audience seated all round, leaving passages through for entrances and exits.

SYNOPSIS OF THE DANCE-MIME

Before the creation there was darkness and a void. To achieve this effect the hall should be in darkness and silence for a few seconds. Into the blackness appears the beginnings of light. To a slight noise of bell, symbol or drumbeat, a small light appears, giving the impression of a star.

The light brightens and the light of day appears, pushing away the powers of darkness. One dancer in a white or light-coloured leotard or costume moves around the arena pushing darkness away as the light increases.

The sea heaves and the land pushes up from the depths of the ocean. Dancers, who had already taken up positions, move from their positions, lying on the ground to represent the land pushing itself above the waters.

The Sun and the Moon next appear, encircling the earth; in majestic procession around the earth and each other. The Sun and Moon are danced by individual dancers and their character can be suggested by dress, masks or by a simple emblem on a short stick which they carry.

Great monsters move ponderously from the waters and roam the earth. Winged creatures fill the sky. Splendid opportunity for impressive movement to music such as excerpts from *The Planets, Night on the bare mountain.*

Beasts begin to roam over the earth.

Man and Woman appear. A period of harmony as all creatures live in peace with each other and serve the Man and Woman.

Man takes the apple and a period of discord ensures, creature fighting with creature. Man and Woman are thrust out.

A joyful sound is heard, the star processes round and is later followed by the Man and Woman, but now the Woman holds a baby in her arms and the costumes suggest Joseph and Mary. The star completes its circle and rests above the family.

The mime ends with a joyful dance and all exit following the Holy Family.

This same dance-mime could be performed to a narration with words taken from the Bible and other sources, giving opportunity for effective choral speaking.

The Ramayana

Mime-Narration based on a Story from the Hindus

The *Ramayana* is a Hindu poem of about 50,000 lines in rhymed metrical couplets. It is an epic poem and not a collection of traditional material. It is considered by the Hindus to be a national treasury of inspired work.

In the story, of which only a small part is included in this dramatisation, the great god, Vishnu, makes a human appearance in the guise of Rama, whose character demonstrates the Hindu sensitivity to what India admired most in a man, a king, a husband, a friend or a warrior. At Hindu religious festivals, especially at Dussehra and Diwali, extracts from the *Ramayana* were recounted at length and it became traditional to act out some of the drama. Emphasis is laid on character portrayal rather than the events, and by the sincerity of the players, the performances, in a simple setting, evoke an emotional response from the audience.

I am suggesting here that the story is read by narrators to an initial tableau with some movement to illustrate the narrative. To assemble the tableaux there is no necessity to provide a front curtain which would be distracting. There is scope for including a number of players and readers in this adaptation of part of the *Ramayana*. Costume, if used, should be colourful and simple, based on the sari for girls and loose coat and trousers for boys.

TABLEAU King Dasaratha with his three wives kneeling before him. Servants in attendance with cup bearer.

NARRATOR In the fertile plains north of the river Ganges, King Dasaratha ruled over the 'unconquerable' city. His fame spread over three worlds, his city was prosperous and his people were happy. His great enemy was a wicked spirit called Ravana and his great sorrow was that he had no son. The great god Vishnu appeared to Dasaratha and told him to give a divine drink to each of his wives and then he, Vishnu the great god, would be born as four sons to Dasaratha. Their names were Rama, Bahrat, Lakshman and Satrughna.

TABLEAU The four sons try to shoot with the great bow of Shiva, the Lord of sleep, tears, anger and deadly fire.

NARRATOR A neighbouring king, King Janak, had a beautiful daughter, Princess Sita, and he promised that she should marry whoever could bend the great bow of Shiva, which had never been bent by any man before. The princes tried in turn, but for three of the sons of Dasaratha the bow would not bend. Rama took the bow and it bent so that he could fit the arrow. Then, drawing the cord, as the bow bent it broke in two. Preparations were made for the wedding of Rama and Sita.

TABLEAU The wedding. The Sage behind the altar. Rama and Sita kneeling, facing each other, attended.

NARRATOR

Softly came the sweet-eyed Sita – bridal blush upon her brow.

Rama in his manly beauty came to take the sacred vow.

Janak placed his beauteous daughter, facing Dasaratha's son.

Spoke with father's fond emotion and the holy rite was done:

'This is Sita, child of Janak, drearer unto him than life,

Henceforth sharer of thy virtue, be she, Prince, thy faithful wife.'

TABLEAU Rama and Sita, with Rama's half-brother, Lakshman, sadly setting off to exile.

NARRATOR The happiness of the couple was short-lived. As a result of a plot at court, Rama's half-brother Bahrat forced King Dasaratha to banish his son, Rama, for fourteen years. At first Rama would not hear of his wife sharing his dangerous life in the jungle, but he eventually gave in. With her and his half-brother, Lakshman, he set out.

Sita said:

Therefore let me seek the jungle where the jungle-rangers rove,

Dearer than the royal palace, where I share my husband's love,

And my heart in sweet communion shall my Rama's wishes share,

And my wifely toil shall lighten Rama's load of woe and care!'

TABLEAU The jungle. Rama, Sita and Lakshman build their own forest retreat, surrounded by jungle animals and also sometimes beset by Rakshas, vicious, superhuman creatures who terrorised all who lived in the jungle.

NARRATOR Rama, with his wife and half-brother, made a forest hermitage for themselves. They did not fear the tigers and other animals who lived around them; they sometimes had visits from other hermits who lived in the forests and they protected all the people and creatures in the jungle from wicked Rakshas, vicious, supernatural and evil creatures. Soon all the evil creatures were driven off and they lived happily for ten years.

TABLEAU The King of the Rakshas, Ravana, hears of Rama's triumph from his sister Surpanakha.

NARRATOR The King of the Rakshas, named Ravana, lived on an island called Lanka (Ceylon) and his sister, Surpanakha, told him of the bravery of Rama, and how he had cleared all the Rakshas from the jungle. He plotted revenge by capturing Sita and taking her from Rama.

TABLEAU Sita, approached by Ravana, disguised as a Brahmin priest.

NARRATOR Ravana, in disguise, pretending to be a priest, approached Sita when she was alone and flung her into his flying chariot. As they flew over the forests she dropped her jewels one by one to leave a trail. The King of the

Eagles tried to stop the chariot but he was killed by Ravana. Sita was carried over the sea to Lanka.

TABLEAU Rama and his army of monkeys, following the trail of jewels, reach the sea.

NARRATOR Rama and his friends raised a great army of monkeys and followed the trail of Sita's jewels until they reached the sea. How were they to cross over the sea to Lanka? The ocean floor rose up and the great army of animals threw rocks to make a bridge for them to cross.

TABLEAU The battle.

NARRATOR The fighting between the army of Ravana and the army of Rama was fierce, but Rama was helped by the great eagle of Vishnu and Ravana's army was beaten. Rama allowed Ravana to escape with his life and went to find Sita.

TABLEAU Rama and Sita meet in the Asoka grove.

NARRATOR Rama and Sita met in the Asoka grove, but Rama was cold and unfriendly. He felt that she had lived in Ravana's keeping and could not now be a wife to be proud of. Sita was so sad that she wished no longer to live, and in accordance with custom she asked that she should be consigned to the flames of a great fire.

TABLEAU Sita steps into the circle of roaring flame, but the flames do not hurt her and she rises up out of the flames, which die down as she steps out of the circle to be reunited with Rama.

NARRATOR The fire was lit and Sita stepped into it. This she was ready to do to prove her love for her husband. The flames fell back from her, not a flame touched her hair or body. The God of the Fire commanded Rama to take back his true wife, Sita. The fire had proved her perfection.

Witness of our sins and virtues, God of Fire incarnate spake,

Bade the sorrow-stricken Rama back his sinless wife to take.

Rama's forehead was unclouded and a radiance lit his eye,
And his bosom heaved in gladness as he spoke in accents
     high,
Never from the time I saw her in her maiden days of youth,
Have I doubted Sita's virtue, Sita's fixed and changeless
     truth.
I have known her ever sinless – let the world her virtue
     know,
For the God of Fire is witness to her true and changeless
     vow!

Note: The verse narrations are selections from Romesh Dutt's
poetic translation which afford some feeling for the poetic
quality of the work.

The Mystery of the Well

A Playlet based on an Indian story by
Suresh Khatri

This playlet originated in two attractive stories from India about the influence of the 'inner voice', which is a common experience but which is often ignored. The story brings out the power of that 'inner voice' if it is heeded and acted upon.

The action takes place near the well which is the only source of water for the needs of the villagers. The well is owned by a wealthy man and, in times of drought, he severely restricts how much water can be taken from it.

PLAYERS

GOVINDA Formerly a cowherd, now guardian of the well, employed by Malak.

RAKHMA A village girl of the caste group known as Harijan, Children of God. They were formerly known as 'Untouchables'.

A BRAHMIN PRIEST Very high caste gentleman.

MOTHER OF RAKHMA

RAMU A young village boy who left the village to work as a domestic servant in a wealthy city man's house. He is paying a visit to his old home, sporting very modern clothes – jeans and T-shirt.

MAMAR Much-travelled, wise old man of the village.

MALAK The wealthy owner of the well.

VILLAGERS Wanting water from the well.

Govinda is lying in the sun when he sees Rakhma stealthily trying to draw water from the well to fill her small bowl.

GOVINDA Hey, you! Let go of that bucket!

RAKHMA Oh, you! Let me just take a small bowl full. Really, there is not a drop of water in our house. Mother says we could die if we don't have some water soon.

GOVINDA It's no use telling me that. I'll give you a hiding if you don't keep away from the well.

RAKHMA (*sitting defiantly as near the well as she dares*) Go on, then, give me a hiding. I don't care. I shall sit here till I get some water.

Enter the Brahmin with his bowl.

BRAHMIN Well, Govinda. Is everything all right with you?

GOVINDA (*grumbling*) No. I would prefer my old job, looking after the cattle. But my master, Malak, has told me to look after the well and stop thieves and rascals from stealing the water.

BRAHMIN But will you let me have water or not? I have to wash as part of my observance, you know. God wills it.

GOVINDA Why not? My master, Malak, says giving you water will earn him God's blessing, or at least it will prevent the well from running dry.

BRAHMIN Of course it will. God be with you and your master.

The Brahmin ceremonially washes his legs and arms, and pours some water over his head. While he does this he utters a prayer – which is translated in the play.

Isha Wasjam idom sarvam, yatkinchajan jagatyou jagat. Ten tyakten bhunjeecha, ma gridhah kasya swiddhanam.

Mother of Rakhma entering with other villagers.

MOTHER Rakhma, what are you doing? Oh, there you are, just sitting. Why haven't you brought the water? We are all dying of thirst.

RAKHMA How can I get water while Govinda will not let me get near the well?

MOTHER Oh, Govinda, why won't you let us have some water?

GOVINDA I have my orders from my master, Malak. What can I do about it?

MOTHER Do you call that fair? You give the Brahmin pots and pots of water to have a bath and you can't spare a drop for us to drink. We may be Harijans but we are human beings, aren't we?

GOVINDA Yes, yes. I've heard it all before. Go and tell that to Malak.

MOTHER Oh, it's no use. Come along home, Rakhma.

RAKHMA And do what? I'll sit here. At least I get a look at some water here.

Ramu enters with Mamar, looking very smart.

RAMU Hullo, Govinda, my old mate. Have you any water in your well? This poor old chap says he can't get a drop in the whole village.

GOVINDA So what can I do?

RAMU Oh, forget about Malak, the mean old devil. Give this old chap some water. If you'll do that I'll ask you along to have a meal at my house some day.

GOVINDA Ramu! Don't come your old tricks with me. You're full of promises. However, good or bad, my master is still my master and I depend on him.

RAMU (*mocking*) Oh, ho! Here is a man of great principle. The one who faithfully obeys his master. Come on, all of you, take some water for yourselves.

The villagers press forward while Govinda vainly tries to stop them.

GOVINDA Get back. Haven't I said 'No' to you?

RAMU You leave them alone.

In the midst of the struggle Malak comes in.

MALAK What's going on here. (*The villagers fall back.*) Why aren't you keeping good order here, Govinda. What do I pay you for?

GOVINDA I'm fed up with looking after the well. I get nothing but blows and abuse.

MALAK What's happening here?

MOTHER Don't you realise that people are dying of thirst?

MALAK What has that got to do with me? The well is mine. When I realised the drought was coming I sold half my cattle so that I could buy the well. I bought it for myself, not for charity. Now go away or I shall fetch the police.

He turns to Mamar.

Now, Mamar, how are you? What news have you got for us?

MAMAR I have a very interesting story to tell, but why are all these people here?

MALAK Oh, it's like this. All the wells have dried up except this one, and so they think I should share my water with them. But what is this story you have to tell?

MAMAR You will remember my brother, Maruti, and how we quarrelled about which of us was more important in our village.

MALAK I think everyone has heard about that.

MAMAR He is richer than me, so he thought he was the senior man, while I am older and wiser, so I thought myself superior. Well, last week we both went together to a meeting where a holy man talked to us. He talked about our two voices. In each of us there is one voice which tells us to be unselfish and loving, while another voice urges us to please ourselves and not worry about other people's troubles. If we would only listen to the good voice, we were told, we could change ourselves, our lives, our relationships with people and, who knows, perhaps the world.

MOTHER Hey, stop talking over there and give us some water.

Villagers agree.

MALAK Wait a minute, this isn't idle talk. Just listen.

MAMAR Well, we all sat in silence for a while and then my brother turned to me and said, 'He's right, you know. Why have we quarrelled all this time over something that is not important. Do forgive me for being such a stupid fool.'

BRAHMIN What did you say to that?

MAMAR I said, 'Of course', and straightaway we forgot our quarrel and I must say we have been closer friends to each other than ever before. Simply by listening to what that voice inside was saying, and then doing what it said.

MALAK H'm. Well, I don't know that I could ask to be forgiven in front of a lot of strange people.

MOTHER Well, don't worry about that, give us some water. Hey, Mamar, why doesn't he listen to that good voice of yours.

MAMAR But he can't listen to my voice – he must listen to his own. Now take your problem. In the village this is the only water you have got.

RAMU That's right.

MAMAR And everyone wants it. That's what is worrying you, eh Malak?

MALAK Yes – exactly.

MAMAR So, just as we did at our meeting, let us all sit quietly and listen for a guiding voice. That is better than all shouting at once.

GOVINDA That's a good idea. Everyone be quiet – and listen.

They all sit or stand in complete silence.

MAMAR (*after a short while*) Well, did a voice speak?

MALAK If I give water to everyone, the well will dry up in no time.

GOVINDA Well, why not give everyone a little water – share it out?

RAMU It's a funny thing. I had felt like giving you a good hiding, Govinda, but I don't want to now.

MOTHER That's strange, for I had felt like going to Malak's house and setting it on fire, but now I have no wish to do so.

BRAHMIN Strangely, when I had my wash a little while ago, I said a prayer without thinking. Now I know what it was:

The whole universe is filled with God's holy spirit,
What need is there for anything else.'

We are all God's children. Should you not share the water then, Malak?

MAMAR Yes. In the old story of our gods, Sita asked 'What is truly in your heart?' and when Hanuman opened his heart there was the god, Ram. So Malak, if you open your heart, what is there?

MALAK To tell you the truth, I had the thought that the water in the well will dry up only when my heart dries up with selfishness. Otherwise it will never dry up. Perhaps Govinda is right. Why not give everyone a little water? Share it out.

RAMU (*as villagers push forward*) Take it easy. Just because

Malak says 'Yes', don't rush. There is enough water here if everyone takes according to his need and not according to his greed. I'll give you a hand, Govinda, to make sure no water is wasted.

MALAK Bravo. This really is serving the village.

GOVINDA Come on, Rakhma, bring your bowl and we'll fill it up.

MOTHER I can hardly believe my eyes. I really thought we'd have to fight to get water. Each day Rakhma has come home saying, 'No water, no water', and I told her that the selfish ways of people won't change till they die. Now I can say that if selfish people change their ways, the living won't have to die.

Away in a Manger

A Dance-Mime

This has evolved from a piece of work by a group of young people, about twelve to fourteen years. It was inspired by their anger that there was so much open conflict in the world between opposing ideologies and even, apparently, between factions ostensibly holding similar religious beliefs. In particular they were concerned with warring Christians in different parts of the world.

The dance involved two sets, the opponents identified by something in the dress. They used no elaborate costume, merely slacks or jeans and shirts. The opponents could be identified by, say, red or blue sashes, by jackboots or sandals, by differing coloured shirts. This is something any group undertaking this work will discuss.

The theme music was the carol *Away in a Manger* which can be arranged for any kind of ensemble from a few recorders and drums to full orchestra. The best effect is probably from a simple grouping. The carol was arranged as a dominant, aggressive march with loud drumming; as a lilting waltz with pipes and strings; and finally as a Christmas carol in which all the players joined.

The dance opened with the entry of the aggressors, marching to the drum beat, weaving patterns across the arena, largely using direct straight lines with abrupt right or left or about turns. They are halted as the music changes to a lilting tune to which the opponents move, circling and encircling the aggressors, cajoling and subtly threatening at the same time. This alternate pattern is repeated two or three times with the alternate obvious threat from the aggressors and the defence and response of the other group.

The groups find themselves in two groups, one on each side of the arena, the very grouping suggesting opposition. A leader from each group stands confronting the other.

They argue along the lines that each wants only to live in

peace but in their own way. Each wants work for all men, each wants good housing, each wants freedom to worship in their own way. Each wants good education for their children, each wants children to be born into a world of freedom and love. Why cannot they agree, where can they find a common thread to pull them together and not apart?

At this point the melody of *Away in a Manger* is heard, and from the back of the arena a woman, dressed to suggest Mary, the Mother of Jesus, but not a copy of a church statue, moves down and stands between the two groups. She has a baby in her arms.

The groups kneel and sing the carol together. As the carol comes to the last verse the groups intermingle and go off in pairs, one of each group together.

A Miracle Play for Christmas

Adapted from several of the medieval miracle plays

These plays were very simple and direct in their approach, and for that reason I felt that they were very close to the manner in which young people approach play-making. 'Go to Bethlehem,' said the Angel. So they went. Mary had her baby in the stable. So she turns round and there it is. Young people take readily to this simple style with its emphasis on words and feeling rather than a great deal of action. This play could well be spoken to a series of tableaux, the words spoken either by the characters concerned or by voices off stage. Set and costume must be as simple as possible.

Enter Joseph and Mary

JOSEPH

Almighty God in Trinity
I pray Thee, Lord, in Thy great might,
Look down. Thy simple servant see.
Here in this place where we are brought,
Weak and alone.
Grant us a resting-place this night
Within this town.

For now are we in grievous need,
As Thou Thyself the sooth may see;
For here is neither blanket nor bed,
And we are weak and both weary,
    And fain would rest.
Now, gracious God, in Thy mercy,
    Show what is best!

MARY

God will guide us, full well know ye!
Therefore, Joseph, be of good cheer.
In this same place born will He be

That shall us save from sorrows sore,
Both night and morn.
Sir, know ye well, the time is near
When He will be born.

JOSEPH   Then it behoves us bide here still,
Here in this same place all this night.

MARY   Yea, forsooth, that is God's will.

JOSEPH   Then would I fain we had some light,
whatever befall.
It grows right dark unto my sight,
and cold withal.

I will go get us light therefore,
And find some fuel to make a fire.

Joseph goes out.

MARY   Almighty God go you before,
As He is sovereign of all things here,
In His great power!
May He lend me grace now to prepare
For this His hour.
*Mary turns her back on the audience and
kneels by the manger. She takes the baby
from the manger, turns to the audience,
with the baby in her arms, and sits facing
audience.*

MARY   Hail, My Lord God! Hail! Prince of Peace!
Hail, my Father! And hail, my Son!
Hail, God and Man, dwelling in One!
Hail, Thou, through Whose might
All this world was first begun,
Darkness and Light!

*Joseph returns but does not see Mary and
baby.*

JOSEPH

Ah! Lord in Heaven! The weather is cold!
The fearfullest freeze that I ever did feel!
I pray God give succour to them that are old,
And also to them that may be unwell,
    So I may say.
Now, God, be Thou my shelter still,
    As best Thou may!

A star appears before him.

Ah, Lord of All! What light is this
That comes shining thus suddenly?
I cannot say, as I have bliss!
When I have brought this wood to Mary
    Then shall I enquire.
Thanks be to God, the place I see.

Joseph moves across to Mary.

MARY

Ye are welcome, sir!

JOSEPH

Tell me, Mary, how farest thee!

MARY

Right well, Joseph, as has been aye.

JOSEPH

O, Mary! What sweet Thing is on thy knee?

MARY

It is my Son, the sooth to say,
    That is so mild.

JOSEPH
(*kneeling*)

Blessed am I, who am bade this day
    To see this Child.
I marvel mickle at this light
That shineth thus throughout this place.
Forsooth, it is a wondrous sight!

MARY

This has He ordained of His grace,
    My Son and King,
That a star be shining for a space
    at His bearing.

Now, Lord, that all this world shall win –
To Thee, my son, this must I say –
Here is no cradle to lay Thee in.
Therefore, my dear Son, I Thee pray,
    Since it is so,
That in this crib I may Thee lay,
    Between beasts two.

She lays the Child in the manger, and an
ass and an ox stand at each side.

MARY
And I shall wrap Thee, my own dear Child,
With such poor clothes as we may have.

JOSEPH
O Mary, behold these creatures mild!
They make devotions, loving and grave,
    As if they were men!
Forsooth, it seems well and clearly told
    That their Lord they ken.

MARY
O, now sleeps my Son! Blest may He be!
He lies full warm these beasts between.

Tableau of Mary, Joseph, and two animals
at side of manger.

Enter shepherd.

1ST SHEPHERD
Now God, that art in Trinity,
Thou save my fellows and me!
For I know not where my sheep nor they be,
    This night is so cold.

But now to make their hearts light,
Now will I full right
    Stand upon this hill,
And to cry them with all my might –
    Full well my voice they know;
    What ho, fellows! Ho! Ho! Hoo!

Enter two shepherds.

2ND SHEPHERD Hark, Sym, hark, I hear our brother on the hill;
This is his voice, right well I know;
Therefore toward him let us go,
    And follow his voice aright.
See, Sym, see where he doth stand?
I am right glad we have him found!
Brother, where hast thou been so long,
    And it is so cold this night.

1ST SHEPHERD Eh, friend, there came a gust of wind with a mist suddenly,
That forth off my ways went I.

3RD SHEPHERD Brother, look up and behold!
What thing is yonder that shineth so bright?
Aha, now is come the time that old fathers have told,
That in the winter's night so cold
A child of maiden would be born
    In whom all prophecies shall be fulfilled.

1ST SHEPHERD Truth it is without nay,
So said the prophet Isaiah,
That a child should be born of a maid so bright
    In winter night the shortest day
Or else in the middle of the night.

Angels sing a happy carol, Gloria in Excelsis.

3RD SHEPHERD Hark, they sing above in the clouds clear!
Heard I never of so merry a choir.

2ND SHEPHERD *Glory, Gloria in excelsis*, that was their song.
How say ye, fellows, said they not thus?

1ST SHEPHERD That is well said; now go we hence
To worship that child of high magnificence,
And that we may be in his presence.

The shepherds approach and enter the stable.

1ST SHEPHERD   Hail, maid-mother and wife so mild!
As the angel said, so have we found.
I have nothing to present to thy child,
But my pipe; hold, hold, take it in thy hand
Wherein much pleasure that I have found.

2ND SHEPHERD   Now hail be Thou, child, and thy dame!
For in a poor lodging here art Thou laid,
So the angel said and told us Thy name;
Hold, take Thou here my hat on Thy head!

3RD SHEPHERD   Hail be Thou, Lord, over water and land,
For Thy coming we all may make mirth,
Have here my mittens to put on Thy hands,
Other treasure have I none to present Thee with.

MARY   Now herd-men kind,
For your coming
To my child shall I pray,
As He is heaven's King,
To grant you His blessing,
That to His bliss He may ye bring
At your last day.

The shepherds leave.

THE ADORATION OF THE MAGI

1ST KING   Lord God, Leader of Israel,
That would die, man to heal,
Come Thou to us not to conceal
But be our counsellor.

2ND KING

Who all this world shalt make well
And shall be called Emmanuel,
Grant us, Lord, with Thee to dwell
And hear now our prayer.

ANGEL

Ah, rise up ye kings three
And come after me
Into the land of Judee
As fast as you may hie.

The child you seek you shall see
Born of a maiden free
That King of heaven and earth shall be
All man back to buy.

1ST KING

Ah, where is the path of the star?
That light is away from us far.

3RD KING

It were best we enquire
Now we lack the star's fire.
Say, you, that rides there,
Tell us some tiding.

MESSENGER

Tell me, sir, what your wills are.

1ST KING

Canst thou say what place or where
A child is born that crown to bear
And of the Jews be King?

2ND KING

We saw a star shine today
In the east in noble array
And we are come all this way
Out joy here to win.

MESSENGER

Hold your peace, sirs, I you pray,
For if King Herod heard you so say
He would go mad, by my fay,
And fly out of his skin.

3RD KING	And since a King is so near We go to him to enquire.
MESSENGER	You may well see he lives here, In this palace does he dwell.

Messenger leads them into Herod

Tidings, now my lord, I shall tell
That these three kings do tell unto me;
Though whence they be I know not well.
Yonder they stand as you may see.

1ST KING	Sir, we saw the star appear In the East over here.
2ND KING	We saw never none so clear And by its ray we came here.
3RD KING	By prophecies well all know we That a child born should be To rule the people of Judee As we have believed many a year.
HEROD	I am King of Kings, none so keen; I the sovereign, sir, as may be seen, I tyrant, wherever I have been, Take castle, tower and town.
	But go ye forth, ye kings three, And enquire if so it be, And anyway come back here to me For you I hope to feed. And if he be of such degree Him will I honour as also do ye.
1ST KING	We leave, sir, Have good day Till we come again this way.

*The kings leave Herod and process round
to the manger.*

MARY   God have mercy, sir kings, for your goodness!
            By the guiding of the Godhead are ye come.
            May my sweet Son reward you for your gifts,
               And His providence speed your journey
               home!

The kings leave the stable.

ANGEL (*meets them*) King of Taurus, Sir Jaspar!
            King of Araby, Sir Balthasar!
            Melchior, King of Aginare!
               To you now am I sent.
            For fear of Herod fierce and wild
            Into your lands return
            And tell not Herod of this child.

1ST KING   Away, sir kings! Brothers, I pray!
            The voice of an angel I heard in my
               dream.

3RD KING   He bade we should return by the West,
            Lest Herod should falsely us betray!

1ST KING   To do it so, that way is the best.
            That Child that we sought, may He
               guide our way!

Born of David's Line

A Playlet for Christmas

A carol is sung.
Young Shepherd is looking for an errant sheep.

YOUNG SHEPHERD Here boy, here boy, where are you? Hey, Hey, Hey, come on, boy. Oh, there you are, you rascal. I've been searching for you all over the place.

OLD SHEPHERD Have you found him, son?

YOUNG SHEPHERD Yes, he's over here. There's plenty of shelter and good grass here. Trust this little rascal to find it. Bring the rest of the flock over. We can rest here for the night.

3RD SHEPHERD Move along then – Hey, Hey, move along. Well done, young'un, finding that sheep. He always was a wanderer. Now we can keep them all together for the night.

OLD SHEPHERD And a cold night it's going to be. We need to rake up a bit of fire, I think, and huddle round it. Just make sure they are all there, son, while we get a fire going.

3RD SHEPHERD That's the idea. You know the sky is quite bright, although there is not much of a moon. I've never seen such a light in the sky. Are all the sheep there, son?

YOUNG SHEPHERD Yes, every one, all settled down for the night.

OLD SHEPHERD Good, then come along up here and have a bite to eat and something to keep you warm.

3RD SHEPHERD There seemed to me to be more people on the roads than usual. What's bringing them all this way?

YOUNG SHEPHERD Don't you know? Just like I've counted the sheep, the officers in Bethlehem, down the road, are counting people. Everyone whose family came from Bethlehem in the past, has to come to Bethlehem to be counted. That's why all descendants of families in Bethlehem are making their way here.

OLD SHEPHERD So that's what it is. I heard something about

that. I haven't been down to the town yet. Suppose I'd better go tomorrow.

3RD SHEPHERD Me, too. Are they charging money for this?

YOUNG SHEPHERD That comes later. When everyone is registered they will work out how much tax is due. Then you pay. Luckily I'm too young.

OLD SHEPHERD Anyhow, let's get some rest. Young'un, you take first watch. Wake me in two hours.

3RD SHEPHERD I don't know as how I shall get to sleep in this cold. G'night.

A pause while young shepherd sings to himself. Suddenly he looks up as if into a great light.

YOUNG SHEPHERD Hey, wake up. Something's happening. It's the moon or a star or something.

SHEPHERDS What is it – Eli – where's that light coming from? It's too bright even to look at it. It's frightening.

OLD SHEPHERD It must be something terrible. Perhaps it's the end of the world.

YOUNG SHEPHERD Listen, quiet. I can hear a voice speaking as if from the middle of the light.

VOICE Don't be afraid. Listen. I bring news of great joy, a joy to be shared by all people. Today in the town of David a Saviour has been born to you. He is Christ the Lord. And here is a sign for you; you will find a baby wrapped in swaddling clothes and lying in a manger.

Silence for a while.

YOUNG SHEPHERD Did you hear what the voice said?

OLD SHEPHERD I think I did, but my hearing's not as good as it used to be. Perhaps we just imagined it.

3RD SHEPHERD He said something about a baby born in Bethlehem. Perhaps we'd better go down and see.

OLD SHEPHERD What, and leave the sheep? We can't do that.

YOUNG SHEPHERD The voice said 'He is Christ the Lord' and in the scriptures it says that out of Bethlehem will come a Lord who will shepherd the people of Israel. We must go, come on. It's important.

3RD SHEPHERD All right lad, we'll come. The sheep will be

all right for a while. Come on, let's get down to Bethlehem.

OLD SHEPHERD It's probably a wild goose chase, but I'll come. I only hope there are no wolves or sheep thieves about.

The shepherds depart.
Enter Herod and official.

HEROD You say there are messages concerning three strangers travelling from the East who have been asking about an audience with me. Who are they? What do they want?

OFFICIAL From all the reports that have preceded them, they appear to be men of learning and of some wealth. They have fine horses and many servants and we are informed that they are looking for a royal boy child.

HEROD Well, they won't find a royal babe here. I have sons enough and when I die my kingdom will be divided between three of them. I don't think any one of them is capable of keeping the kingdom together.

OFFICIAL That is indeed so, your Majesty. The people have much to thank you for.

HEROD I have tried to preserve a balance between Jew and Pagan even when it has meant ruthless action. Now you say these three visitors seek a new king.

OFFICIAL Yes, sire. This could mean danger. Will you see them when they come?

HEROD Yes. Keep me informed and send for me as soon as they arrive, that is, if they indeed come at all. Have you made all necessary arrangements for taking the census ordered by the Emperor Octavian?

OFFICIAL Yes, sire, all people have been ordered to report to the town of their former lineage. Officers have been posted to administer the census.

HEROD Good. Keep a close watch on this and let me know should those three strangers arrive.

Exit Herod and official.
Enter three Magi (Wise Men).

1ST MAGI We must enquire at Herod's palace about the Babe. The prophecy foretells the birth of a Royal child and it is here in this palace in Jerusalem that the royal family live. From my readings the child will grow to be a great Lord and King. That is why I bring gold to present to him, a gift symbolising royal authority.

2ND MAGI You may be right, but I bring frankincense, for my studies tell me that the child will be a great High Priest, a man of God, indeed it would seem that he will be God himself.

3RD MAGI I can agree with you both to some extent but it would seem to me that this child, of whom many ancient prophecies speak, will be a Saviour of mankind, almost a sacrifice for the wrongdoings of men. I have brought myrrh, foretelling the possibility of death, the glory of death as a sacrifice for others.

2ND MAGI Well, here we are in the palace of Herod; will he see us, that's the point?

1ST MAGI Here comes a palace official. He will know.

Enter official.

OFFICIAL Gentlemen, you are welcome indeed. King Herod knows of your coming, for a message was received giving us news of you.

1ST MAGI We were delayed a little. We had all journeyed from different parts and only recently have we come together. Will King Herod see us?

OFFICIAL He will indeed. He is greatly interested in your mission. Here he comes.

HEROD Gentlemen, you are welcome. What news have you of this child?

3RD MAGI We were hoping that you would have news for us, my lord. The child we seek is a royal babe and it seemed fitting to us that we first look for him in the royal palace.

HEROD But I have no new child. Indeed it is many years now since a child was born to me. Are you sure of your facts?

2ND MAGI The message written in the skies is clear. We have worked on this for two years, ever since the star first appeared.

HEROD A star? What star? What are you talking about.

1ST MAGI This new star in the firmament was first observed

in the Eastern sky nearly two years ago. We studied its early progress in conjunction with the constellations and concluded that this was to lead us to the One foretold in the ancient prophecies, 'The Prince of Peace'.

2ND MAGI 'Emmanuel', which means God with us.

3RD MAGI 'A man of sorrows', the one whose side will be pierced.

HEROD (*to official*) What are these men talking about? I have no child, yet they talk as if the child is already born. (*To Magi*) I don't understand you. What else is said of the child?

1ST MAGI He will be a leader of men. A son of David.

HEROD Is that so? Then you must look for him in the town of David. Bethlehem is the place you want. Go and find out all you can about this child and be sure to come back and tell me all about him. I would like to visit him and do homage to such a child. You say the star has been apparent for two years?

2ND MAGI Yes, Your Majesty. This journey has indeed been a wearisome and arduous time. But now it seems we are nearing the end. Come, fellow travellers, let us make our way to Bethlehem in Judah. Good-day, Your Majesty.

MAGI Good-day, Your Majesty. Peace be with you.

HEROD Peace be with you, my friends. Do not forget to return and tell me of what you find in Bethlehem.

Magi go

HEROD (*to official*) Tell the officers of the palace legion to prepare two cohorts for stand-by duty. I think there will be business to be done in Bethlehem.

Herod and official depart.
Enter innkeeper and wife.

INNKEEPER I tell you, we can't take any more people in. We already have more than the regulations allow. And then there's the food. If we take any more, everyone will have to go short, and then there will be trouble about payments. If the Roman officers come round and find that we are over our quota, we shall have fines to pay.

WIFE All right, all right. I took that last couple in because they were so old and tired. I don't know who thinks up these rules and regulations. Why should everyone have to travel back to the family town in order to be counted? Just another rule to impress on us that the Romans govern the country.

INNKEEPER Well, whatever the reason, we are now full up. 'No vacancies', and don't be soft and get taken in by some sob story. We dare not let anyone else stay here.

WIFE If you say so, although I would be sorry for anyone who had to sleep out. It looks like being a bleak night, one of the coldest of the year.

INNKEEPER I'll get on with the wood cutting – there'll be need of plenty with all the folks we have.

He goes out.

WIFE This place wants a good cleaning up (*sweeps*). I can see there are some travellers still out on the road. Poor souls, they are in for a cold night. That couple look as though they can't go much farther. Goodness, they are coming here.

Joseph and Mary approach.

JOSEPH Excuse me, but can you tell me where we can get a room for the night?

WIFE Oh dear. I don't think I can. We have already taken in more guests than we are allowed. We daren't take any more.

JOSEPH We are late because we could only journey slowly. I've called at many places but they are all full up. 'Sleep out in the hedgerow', they say, but you can see that my wife is in no state to sleep out in the open. Our baby will be born very soon.

WIFE Yes, I can see; but I daren't let you in. I wouldn't mind the soldiers, but my husband.... Oh dear, he would be very cross. The truth is the other guests wouldn't give up their rooms or share them.

JOSEPH Mary, dear, I am afraid we'll have to go on. They have no room at the inn.

They turn to go away.

WIFE Look, would the stable be all right? We're not supposed
to put people in it, but it's quite clean just now ... there's
only a donkey in it. We could tie him up and leave you quite
a bit of room. There's plenty of clean straw and I could
find a blanket or two. Do you think you could manage?

MARY I am sure we can. You are very kind to go to all this
trouble, especially since you are so busy. Come, Joseph,
let us stop here for the night. I am sure we shall be comfortable. Are you sure your husband won't mind?

WIFE Oh, I expect he'll grumble a bit, but I can deal with him.
Come on in. If you ask me, your baby is just about due.
I'll see that you have everything you need.

They go out back stage.
A carol is sung.
Enter Wife, Joseph and Mary with babe.

WIFE Come on in here, dear, and sit quietly with your little
son.

MARY Thank you. You have been so kind, and the Inn is so full
of your guests.

WIFE Oh, I let my husband get on with them and the girl
who helps in the kitchen knows what to do. Most things
were got ready beforehand. Now are you comfortable there?

MARY Yes, indeed. Weren't we lucky, Joseph, to find some-
where like this? It all seemed to be planned.

JOSEPH That is so. Ever since that day, so many months ago,
when I was told in a dream that our son was to be some-
body special. It seems that our footsteps have been guided
to this place.

WIFE Yes, your wife was telling me about those dreams. (*Goes
to door.*) What are you folk doing out there? We've no
room for you.

IST SHEPHERD We don't want room. We believe that a baby
has been born here and we have come to worship him.

YOUNG SHEPHERD We were out in the field when a great light
appeared in the sky and a voice told us not to be afraid
but that a child was to be born who would be our Saviour.

The voice told us to go to Bethlehem and find the child in a stable.

2ND SHEPHERD Yes, and we heard voices singing, 'Glory to God'. Is there a baby here?

WIFE Indeed there is. Wait a minute. (*To Mary*) There are some shepherds out here wanting to see your baby. Do you want them to come in?

MARY Yes, let them come.

WIFE Well, you can come in for a minute, but you mustn't tire the baby's mother. Step in quietly.

Shepherds enter.

YOUNG SHEPHERD This is exactly what we were told in the fields. 'You shall find the babe wrapped in swaddling clothes, lying in a manger'.

JOSEPH So much of what has happened has been foretold. Yet I am afraid for the future. I have a premonition of danger and it may not be safe for us to stay here too long.

2ND SHEPHERD God be with you, blessed family. Our own experience tells us that this is no ordinary babe, yet why this is so is still a mystery. We must get back to our work with the sheep in the fields.

MARY Thank you all for coming.

WIFE Now off you go quietly. The Mother and her child need rest and quiet.

The shepherds go, passing the Magi, who approach. Young shepherd stays to listen to them.

1ST MAGI The star has led us to Bethlehem and now stands over the village inn. I find that very strange, for how can a royal babe be born in a small country inn? Perhaps we have made mistakes in our predictions. There is a light in the stable. There is a woman bending over a manger, there is a baby too. The woman is singing quietly to herself. This is the place we have been seeking. Listen.

Mary sings: 'My soul doth magnify the Lord'.

1ST MAGI There – I foretold that this babe would be a Lord and King; for that reason I brought my gift of gold.

Mary sings: 'And my spirit doth rejoice in God'.

2ND MAGI As I told you, the babe would be a great High Priest identified with God. I was right to bring frankincense.

Mary concludes: 'In God, my Saviour'.

3RD MAGI I saw the babe as a sacrifice and Saviour of men. That was the significance of my gift of myrrh.

1ST MAGI Dear Lady, may we enter to present our gifts to your son?

MARY Yes, you are all welcome.

WIFE Not too much fuss, please. The mother needs rest and quiet. Come in just for a little while.

Magi enter. Young shepherd hides in the corner and listens.

1ST MAGI I present gold, representing the power of earthly kingship and for the good of the people.

2ND MAGI I bring frankincense, representing the mystic forces of the spirit.

3RD MAGI I give myrrh, foretelling sacrifice and death, freely given so that men achieve eternal life.

1ST MAGI Our good wishes and congratulations, good lady.

They leave the stable, followed by young shepherd, unobserved.

3RD MAGI I confess I am bewildered. Can this babe, born so modestly, really be the fulfilment of all the prophecies?

2ND MAGI Will Herod believe us if we go back and tell him that his King is a child born of very humble parents in the stable of a country inn!

1ST MAGI I sense danger here. Herod will take no chances. He was so insistent that we should go back to him and report whatever we found.

3RD MAGI Too insistent, I believe. Let us return to our homes and forget Herod's instruction to give him news of what we have found. Our journey has been significant. We must do nothing that might bring harm to the child.

Magi go.
Young shepherd returns to stable and listens to the next conversation.

JOSEPH Mary, we must get away from this place. (*To wife*) We are grateful to you for giving us this shelter while the child was born, but it is in my mind that there is danger for us if we stay.

WIFE You are welcome to stay longer if you please. I'll see no harm comes and I'll keep out any other visitors.

JOSEPH The visitors sent by Herod will not be kept out. They will bring death and sorrow, but they must not find the child. Mary, we must make our way over the frontier into Egypt. There we shall be safe from any harm that Herod could do.

MARY If you say so, Joseph. Come, let us prepare for the journey. Our faithful donkey who brought us here from Nazareth must now carry us into Egypt. (*She notices the young shepherd.*) You, lad, will you help us to get away from Bethlehem quickly?

YOUNG SHEPHERD Indeed, I will. I know a path made by the sheep which will take you round the village and away on to the road to Egypt. I'll carry that bundle. Your donkey is tied up just down this road.

MARY Let us hurry, Joseph, and stay in Egypt until it is safe for us to go home.

WIFE Goodbye, and God keep you all.

(*Joseph, Mary and shepherd go.*)

End with a carol.

The Lord's Prayer

A Dance-Mime

A new emphasis can often be imparted to a familiar prayer or psalm if it is acted out as it is spoken. This should give all members of the group the opportunity of contributing to the discussion that is aroused and will often bring home the meaning of a word or a phrase that has not hitherto been apparent, in spite of the number of times the prayer has been recited. The Lord's Prayer is an example of this, for many are the humorous stories which illustrate the fact that a child may have repeated a line of the prayer scores of times but has nevertheless not fully understood what he has been saying. 'Harold be thy Name' is perhaps the supreme, oft-quoted example. The true meaning has been squeezed out with so much repetition. A misunderstanding of this sort could not occur if the prayer had been analysed to accompany appropriate movement.

What follows here should not be taken as a blue-print for this work, with a teacher acting as controller or director. Detail is worked out here only to present ideas to the inexperienced teacher. What finally emerges will be the work of the group, original and stimulating, for it will have come out of the players' experience and interchange of ideas with a great deal of experiment preceding it. When completed the young people involved will have a far deeper understanding of the prayer itself. After the first experience, the group will be able to treat other prayers, poems or psalms with a similar technique. I use the traditional 'Prayer Book' form of the prayer, but the class may well prefer one of the more modern versions.

It is suggested that one group work on the choral speaking whilst a second group experiment with the accompanying movement. Each should supplement and support the other.

'Our Father, Our Father, Our Father'

The spoken words can be built up from one or two voices for the first, 'Our Father', additional voices strengthening the second and third repeats.

In a similar fashion the movement group can underline this by entering one-third of their number at a time. The posed groups can be sculptured with lying, kneeling, sitting and standing figures.

'Which art in heaven'

A possible illustrative movement would be to allow the centre group to extend upwards to the full height of one central player with one or both arms extended upwards. To strengthen such a move, every eye should follow the move to its full height.

'Hallowed be Thy Name'

The three sub-groups adopt reverent attitudes. There might be some discussion about the meaning of 'hallowed' and 'reverent'. Common attitudes would be a 'hands together' at prayer or palms of hands across the chest, but the performers will probably present original ideas.

'Thy Kingdom come'

The strength of this petition could well be emphasised by the three movement sub-groups joining in a circular form either looking out or all looking inwards to central figure or figures. Use variety in height and width in the shapes created by the figures, grouped in pairs, threes or more.

'Thy will be done on earth'

The theme of this grouping could be submission, not servile but willing, with the feeling of power from above. In all these sections the speaking chorus can repeat the petition adding variety by pace, modulation and by the number of voices used.

'As it is in Heaven'

A tremendous expression of uplift and fulfilment. The change of mood from the previous petition has considerable dramatic effect.

'Give us this day our daily bread'

This petition is practical and the general picture will be of asking and giving. Some players will work in pairs, some in larger groups with the emphasis on attitudes of supplication and rewarding.

'Forgive us our trespasses as we forgive those who trespass against us'

Once more the antithesis will be made clear between those wronged and those forgiving. There might well be a central theme representing an incident which underlines God's forgiveness. This could be a group hinting at the Prodigal Son, or some other example of God's forgiveness as shown in a parable or incident.

'And lead us not into temptation'

The repetition of the word 'temptation' by voices in the choral group can be very effective; warning, seductive, menacing, and so on with reaction from the movement group.

'But deliver us from evil'

There is opportunity in this line for reaction from the tempted, a rejection of the temptation and a withdrawal of the tempter, all underlined by the speaking group.

'For Thine is the Kingdom'

After the climax of the previous petition allow the mood to drop both vocally and visually so that the final climax will be the more effective. Make this grouping generally low, figures kneeling or lying at floor level.

'The Power and the Glory'

Once more voices and figures look upward and move upward with considerable force demonstrated by the lines of groups of bodies and strong eye-lines held by players within each sub-group.

'For ever and ever'

Gain as much height as possible with voices and figures. Experienced members of the group may even include a figure lifted off the floor to achieve height and again strengthen this with strong eye-lines from all the players. The choral group can make much of the phrase 'and ever' by repetition, always looking for variety.

'Amen'

Give a great deal of thought to this final tableau and the delivery of the 'Amen'. Is it more effective to sound a great 'Amen' or to give this word to one clear voice?

It is evident that this work is very individual and the final shape will be the outcome of a great deal of discussion leading to a greater understanding of this prayer, which suffers from being too familiar.

If this venture proves successful, find further poems, psalms and prayers that can be treated in a similar fashion.

The Daniel Jazz

by Vachel Lindsay

Darius the Mede was a king and a wonder.
His eye was proud, and his voice was thunder.
He kept bad lions in a monstrous den.
He fed up the lions on Christian men.

Daniel was the chief hired man of the land.
He stirred up the jazz in the palace band.
He whitewashed the cellar. He shovelled in the coal.
And Daniel kept a-praying: 'Lord, save my soul.'
Daniel kept a-praying: 'Lord, save my soul.'
Daniel kept a-praying: 'Lord, save my soul.'

Daniel was the butler, swagger and swell.
He ran upstairs. He answered the bell.
And *he* would let in whoever came a-calling:
Saints so holy, scamps so appalling.
Old man Ahab leaves his card.
Elisha and the bears are a-waiting in the yard.
Here comes Pharaoh and his snakes a-calling.
Here comes Cain and his wife a-calling.
Shadrach, Meshach and Abednego for tea.
Here comes Jonah and the whale,
And the *Sea*!

Here comes St Peter and his fishing-pole.
Here comes Judas and his silver a-calling,
Here comes old Beelzebub a-calling.
And Daniel kept a-praying: 'Lord, save my soul.'
Daniel kept a-praying: 'Lord, save my soul.'
Daniel kept a-praying: 'Lord, save my soul.'

His sweetheart and his mother were Christian and meek.
They washed and ironed for Darius every week.

One Thursday he met them at the door:
Paid them as usual, but acted sore.
He said: 'Your Daniel is a dead little pigeon.
He's a good hard worker, but he talks religion.'
And he showed them Daniel in the lions' cage.
Daniel standing quietly, the lions in a rage.

His good old mother cried:
'Lord, save him.'
And Daniel's tender sweetheart cried:
'Lord, save him.'

And she was a golden lily in the dew.
And she was as sweet as an apple on the tree.
And she was as fine as a melon in the corn-field,
Gliding and lovely as a ship on the sea.
And she prayed to the Lord:
'*Send* Gabriel. *Send* Gabriel.'

King Darius said to the lions:
'Bite Daniel. Bite Daniel.
Bite him. Bite him. Bite him!'
Thus roared the lions:
'We want Daniel, Daniel, Daniel.
We want Daniel, Daniel, Daniel.
Grrrrrrrrrrrrrrrrrrrrrrrrrrrrrrrrr
Grrrrrrrrrrrrrrrrrrrrrrrrrrrrrrrrrr,'
And Daniel did not frown,
Daniel did not cry.
He kept on looking at he sky.

And the Lord said to Gabriel:
'Go chain the lions down,
Go chain the lions down,
Go chain the lions down,
Go chain the lions down.'
And *Gabriel* chained the lions,
And *Gabriel* chained the lions,
And *Gabriel* chained the lions,

And Daniel got out of the den,
And Daniel got out of the den,
And Daniel got out of the den.
And Darius said: 'You're a Christian child',
Darius said: 'You're a Christian child'.
And gave him his job again,
And gave him his job again,
And gave him his job again.

This humorous work lends itself to a variety of ways of presentation and whatever the method finally chosen, verse speaking, dramatic, dance or mime, with or without musical or percussion accompaniment, it will always be unique to the group presenting it.

The story of Daniel should be studied from a text dependent upon the age and maturity of the class. There is a wide range to choose from. *Bible Stories* by David Kossof has the story in very readable form, but it is also worth reading the same story in one of the more modern Bible translations, say *The Jerusalem Bible*. This study will give a setting for the Daniel Jazz. Some discussion of Negro spiritual tradition will help before getting down to reading the Jazz and deciding on the form in which it is to be presented. Certainly it asks for something more imaginative than a straightforward choral speaking.

After a first reading all will appreciate the beat of the lines and the group might read it again with hand clapping to emphasise the changes in rhythm. The clapping is often 'off-beat', to use a jazz expression.

The poem can then be broken up with groups of voices holding conversations back and forward, single voices or small groups picking out phrases like 'Lord, save my soul', 'Lord, save him', 'You're a Christian child'. (Was he a Christian child? If not, why did the poet put that line in?) The lines roared by the lions, 'We want Daniel', seem to call for chants like those shouted by cheer groups at American ball games. The lions' roar 'Grrrrrrrr' offers a lovely speech exercise in tongue management. There are many more opportunities for making this a very exciting choral item.

There is so much action and so many well-defined characters that many will want to dramatise the poem, miming actions with a speaking chorus telling the story.

Remembering its 'Negro spiritual' origin, the costume can be imaginative. Darius, to denote his superiority, may wear a top hat and tails, somewhat battered and worn, and other characters can reflect in costume, the Deep South.

Break into the poem on occasions to give the mime artists time to develop their contribution. For instance, after 'He stirred up the jazz in the palace band', a strangely dressed 'kazoo' band could be led by Daniel, in Majorette style playing a modern, appropriate 'pop' tune, before Daniel gets down to his 'whitewashing' and 'coal-shovelling'.

If the silence from the choral speakers while such actions are going on is found to be worrying or difficult, they can fill in with clapping or tapping or even humming a suitable melody quietly.

The procession of callers offers the opportunity of amusing extravagant costume – how do you dress 'the Sea'? And again take time over this to achieve greatest effect.

The beat of this poem suggests percussion accompaniment, elaborate or simple as you please – drums, bongoes, cymbals. To avoid the monotony or the regular beat, experiment with changes in rate. 'His sweetheart and his mother' can be taken at a slower rate than the preceding verse. 'And she was a golden lily' etc. has another, different, 'blues' rhythm.

For a teacher looking for a project theme, *The Daniel Jazz*, with Biblical origin, its American history setting, its Christian reference, its opportunity for art, music and drama experimentation, affords work for several weeks, perhaps half a term.

Saint Joan

A Mime-Drama

This piece of work arose from a Teachers' Course on Drama in Religious Education. It was my practice, when conducting such courses, to work during the same period of time with a class of children of the appropriate age range, employing the same techniques at a different intellectual level. Then, at the final session of the course, the children did their work for the teachers and vice versa. This method gave rise to a great deal of useful discussion between the two groups and on occasions a request from the children to try out the work presented by the teachers.

On this particular teachers' course, the class of children, aged eight to nine years, were working on 'The Seasons', which is described in detail on page 25, the theme being the natural cycle of life, death, life again, which in itself afforded considerable material for discussion. The teachers then decided to take a similar theme of a life which seemed to end tragically and disastrously, but in fact was a life that continues to be influential centuries after the actual death. While 'The Seasons' provoked some discussion on the nature of death, the teachers also found the life of St Joan a talking point, centred on the nature of sacrifice, giving one's life for a principle, and eventually on the life and sacrifice of Jesus.

The teachers on their drama course considered that a playlet would inhibit the development of the story of Joan's life and that some elements needed an expression of mood rather than story-telling in words. A mime which took the story along, as well as affording opportunity to express moods, was their choice; for want of a better title they called it a 'mime-drama', but what's in a name? The work that emerged could well be performed by pupils at the upper end of the age range we are considering.

The story was divided into the following elements:

1. The farm workers.
2. The English victories.
3. The call to Joan.
4. Joan leads the French.
5. The capture of Joan.
6. Martyrdom.

The episodes were performed with suitable musical background but could well be accompanied by a rhythm and recorder group. This will depend on how much time is to be allotted to the work and the talent of the group. Even the least musical of the children can be responsible for effective percussion accompaniment.

1. *The farm workers.* This consisted of miming appropriate actions to a background of music with a somewhat rustic character. In this case the teachers picked out parts of Beethoven's 6th Symphony, *The Pastoral.* Suitable mime can be developed by each performer, such as mowing with a scythe, raking, sowing, reaping, binding, gleaning, and so on. We were not so pedantic as to say that not all these things go on simultaneously on a farm. Nor is it necessary to have a great number of performers to make the mime effective. In most dramatic work it is beneficial to have space rather than crowded areas.

2. *The English victories.* An ominous note is struck as drum beats are heard in the distance. The farm workers move fearfully away from the centre as from the end of the arena soldiers, French and English, take up opposite stations. To a musical background, a battle is fought out in mime. There does not have to be a crowded mêlée; even as few as four or five on each side can make an effective battle. The players should not make physical contact but each one should be clear in his mind as to what weapon he is using, how heavy it is, how it is held and used and so on. The battle can be fought as duels, but it is better if there is movement between the groups. Eventually the French flee the field and the English group finish as a triumphant tableau at one end of the arena. The music used by the

group I have mentioned was an excerpt from *Rite of Spring* by Rimsky Korsakov.

3. *The Call to Joan.* The peasants return to the fields, shaken and disconsolate, and continue their work with little enthusiasm. (Music *Cold Winter* by Sibelius.) The music fades as we hear the tolling of the church bell. Joan looks towards the church, and after listening for a moment or two moves to one end of the arena and picks up a sword which she holds above her head aggressively.

4. *Joan leads the French.* To rousing music (not a march, for that is too restrictive) she rouses the French troops and leads them spiritedly to occupy the centre of the arena forming a tableau facing outwards. The English troops return and the battle is resumed. The French are this time victorious and they move off with the obvious intention of celebrating the victory, leaving Joan alone at prayer. The musical excerpt used for this was from the last part of *Scheherezade* by Rimsky Korsakov. The storm music served for the battle and the end of the tumult; the *Scheherezade* theme on the violin underlined the quiet serenity of Joan.

5. *The capture of Joan.* The withdrawal of the French soldiers from Joan, leaving her alone at the mercy of the menacing advance of two or three English soldiers who capture her and take her away, was quietly accompanied by percussion instruments, moving to a crescendo as Joan is bound to a post holding her sword in front of her— now representing a cross.

6. *Martyrdom.* All the players now surround Joan on their knees and crouching down. As the fire burns and the flames leap up, the players represent the flames, moving up and down with the whole body, arms outstretched and flickering to suitable music. *Ritual Fire Dance* or *Prince Igor Dances* are effective pieces for this. The effect is spoiled if the dancers' movements are too uniform. Each must work as an individual, swaying, turning and using whole body and arm movement. The music fades and Joan, who has slumped in death, now lifts high in front of her the cross (represented by the hilt of the sword) and as

triumphant music rings out, Joan moves through the flames and goes out, followed by the other players.

This mime-drama lends itself to considerable ingenuity and individuality. It is essential to tape the chosen pieces of music used in sequence, so that each episode moves fluently into the next.

Spit Nolan

Improvisation inspired by a short story by
Bill Naughton

Short stories are often a valuable source of material for
dramatisation in some form and in work with young people
it is obviously advisable to look for extracts from collections
of short stories written for the age group. Bill Naughton's
book, *The Goalkeeper's Revenge – and other stories* is such
a source, for these are stories about boys and girls, for young
people of about 11 years and over. Subjects for young people
of this age need not avoid sadness. Acting out stories can help
young people to come to terms with the fact that life is not
all fun and games, but that families have to encounter sad
happenings. Such a story is *Spit Nolan*.

Briefly, Spit Nolan is a thin, ill-nourished lad from the
poorer quarter of a northern city, suffering from a lung
disease that is gradually killing him. One of the more important
activities in the crowded area of the town where Spit lives is
'trolley-carting', and Spit is recognised as the champion of his
district. Trolleys are go-carts made from a wooden box nailed
or bolted to a long plank, to which four wheels are attached.
The front two wheels are attached to a wooden spar which
acts as an axle which can be pivoted to enable the driver to
steer. Refinements like ball-bearings, strings and straps for
guiding the cart, a back rest to the driver's seat and so on are
optional and varied. Indeed, the source of much of the
material used by the 'go-carters' is something that does not
bear too close an inspection. Many a scrap dealer has wondered where the wheels of an old 'pram' went to overnight.
The venue for competition on these vehicles is 'The Brew', a
steep road leading down to the cemetery with a sharp turn
at the bottom which had to be negotiated skilfully to avoid
driving the cart into the traffic in a busy street.

Spit, in spite of his ill-health, is the unbeaten champion on
this course and is inevitably idolised by the girls and admired

or envied by the boys. All trolleys have names and Spit's vehicle is called 'Egdam'. The name of his favourite girl is embodied here.

Then a 'clever dick' turns up to challenge Spit. He is the son of a local publican and has had his 'trolley' purpose-built for him at a local engineering works.

Inevitably they race before a record crowd of supporters, but at the end of the thrilling encounter Spit's machine runs out of control into the path of an oncoming charabanc. It will be necessary to translate this into 'coach' for present-day youngsters.

The ambulance arrives to carry Spit away and as he is put into it, the truth dawns on the silent crowd of young people as the nurse asks, 'Where did he live?'

When I used this material at a Teachers' Course on Religious Drama, I read the story to a group of children in the morning session and asked them to imagine that they were characters in the story. The boys should think out every detail of their home and family as characters in the story and know exactly what their own trolley looked like, how they acquired the materials, how they made the wheels run better, how they polished the boards, how they guided the cart and so on. The girls became supporters and girl friends, so that the group achieved a total relationship as well as individual personalities. We worked out how we could make the race look impressive and real, although the action must be contained in the centre of a school hall. It was appreciated that while two carts ran alongside at speed, there need be no movement between them at all – the carts, of course, were imaginary. If one 'cart' stayed still the other had only to 'inch' ahead or behind to give reality to the race. The main characters, Spit, Madge, the newcomer, the ambulance driver, the charabanc driver and the nurse, were individually cast.

During the morning session with the class, conversation led inevitably to the nature of death, the unfairness of life and speculation on 'why' do tragedies happen, why are they 'allowed' to happen.

When the teachers on the course met, after school, and at

the school of the class concerned, I told them briefly what
the class of young people had done and then brought the boys
and girls in. They each set about preparing the 'go-carts' for
practice. The teachers mingled among them and talked to
them about what they were doing and the boys and girls
explained to them exactly what a 'go-cart' was, what their
own 'go-cart was like and also told the teachers on a one-to-
one basis, the story of Spit Nolan.

The young group then performed their own version of *Spit
Nolan*. Bill Naughton would have recognised it, but they
had added a great deal of their own experience, especially
regarding relationships, the rivalries, the friendships, the co-
operation, but above all their concern for Spit Nolan. The
race was acted out and Spit Nolan's body was taken off in the
ambulance. With a show of varying reactions, the group
broke up determined to go on 'carting' because Spit would
have wanted them to.

When the young players had been duly thanked and sent off
home, the teacher group discussed the work. There was some
curiosity, mingled with criticism, that I had chosen a story
with a death in it. This is, of course, a matter of opinion,
but I was encouraged when one of the teachers told us that
the young boy who had been telling her about Spit Nolan had
explained all this to her. Evidently, he had explained that,
in a way, Spit's death was fortuitous, since he was very
ill anyway, and if he had lived on and become more and
more ill he wouldn't have been able to continue with his go-
carting, and in that case he would have not wanted to live.
Better to die in these circumstances than live on in pain
and ill-health, unable to enjoy life in the way he wanted
to.

This seemed to me to be an example of what I am sure is
true, that through dramatic activity young people, and old
come to that, can come to terms with difficult situations and
relationships.

The story of Spit Nolan can be approached through Drama
in a number of ways, but I would recommend it to teachers
with boys and girls in the 10–12 age group.

In the same book I would recommend a story entitled *The*

Well-Off Kid. Pupils of 10–12 years old are quite capable of taking this and making it into an effective playlet. It looks simply, but with great effect, into what being 'well-off' really means.

Holy Spirit

An Improvisation

One of the more time-consuming aspects of preparing an improvisation is gathering together the poems, stories, comments and so on that are truly relevant. Very rarely does one find all that one needs within the covers of one book. Such a book, I suggest, is *Come, Holy Spirit* by Peter de Rosa. Here is a store of verse and prose comment, illustration and anecdote that affords ample material for a group of young people to present in the form of an improvisation. More than that, in working together to present the concepts set out in the book, in the form of mime, dance, speech and appropriate sound and music, the players will come closer to an understanding of what the Holy Spirit means to each of them as an individual. It is an exciting and colourful book and the resulting work should be colourful, including touches of humour that highlight the serious intent of the work.

The presentations might begin with processional entry to the words, spoken or chanted, of one of the well-known Whitsun hymns, say 'Come, Holy Ghost'. Interspersed between the verses, one or two of the lovely stories told by Peter de Rosa in his introduction could be used with a lead into the current use of Hawks and Doves in modern politics, the Doves being messengers of peace.

This peaceful reference might give place to a short enactment of the old 'Whitsun Ale' celebrations in parishes in former times, the carousel being ended by the Minister firmly reminding his unruly flock that Whitsun is the time of beginning with new spirit, power and authority. A reminder of the origin of White Sunday is presented by figures in white coming to be baptised.

The use of Water gives a lead back to references in Peter de Rosa's second chapter which illustrate the symbolism of water for the Holy Spirit. Some of the quotations from the

Old Testament lend themselves to dance to a choral speech background.

Possibly here short dramatic scenes could underline the value of water in the desert, the story of Jesus and the Samaritan woman at the well, and a passing reference to Jesus' cry from the Cross, 'I thirst'. Drama here can underline the truth that Jesus was thirsting not only for water.

The likeness of the Holy Spirit to the Wind can be presented very actively in dance and will give an opportunity to the sound effects team to provide original backing. The mystery, the power, the fearsomeness of the wind are exciting subjects, reaching a climax in the words from the *Book of Acts*: 'Suddenly a sound came from heaven like the rush of a mighty wind and it filled all the house where they were sitting.'

The Holy Spirit is next likened to Fire and possibly more than anything else, Fire gives opportunity for dance and mime. It is not difficult to introduce 'fire' colours of reds, blues, yellows and so on, even by such a simple device of giving each dancer a long strip of coloured material which will swirl up and down and round the dancer. Use music like *Ritual Fire Dance* or *Prince Igor Dances* or, even as Peter de Rosa mentions, 'Keep the home fires burning'. But in the excitement of all this movement do not forget the theme, and insert episodes in which God reveals himself in Fire and Flame, with quotations such as John the Baptist's, 'He will baptize you with the Holy Spirit and Fire.'

A calmer interlude after the Storms and the Fire will underline the likeness between the Holy Spirit and Oil. Perhaps the most obvious reference that could easily be included is found in the 23rd Psalm.

The improvisation can be brought to an end with a return to a Whitsun hymn or a dance-mime improvised on Gerard Manley Hopkins' *God's Grandeur*.

One of the arts of presenting an improvisation is to link the separate components so that they make an entity and do not appear as unconnected items. This means that there should be no commentator introducing the elements but that the theme or message will be self-evident.

Fings Ain't What They Used To Be

Improvisation for Experienced Older Groups

Constructing and performing an improvisation gives a group of young people the opportunity to explore in depth matters of concern to them. This is Religious Education in its widest sense, for it is a statement of truths that are common to most faiths; concern for others and help for the less fortunate; impatience with hypocrisy; a desire to end unfairness, poverty, cruelty and conflict. Young people will choose their own themes and the two presented here are no more than patterns which will hopefully prove to be useful as starting points. The source material for such work is limitless: stories, poems, plays, newspaper articles, songs, music, sounds and so on.

Experienced groups may experiment with spontaneous rather than prepared improvisation, being given limited time in which to present their comments and attitudes towards a given theme.

The first theme is inspired by the frustration that arises from seeing huge tracts of our countryside despoiled by the onward march of motorways, huge factories polluting the air, old and beautiful buildings shaken by massive container lorries and all the other features of modern life that are so unbeautiful. This drastic change that has come about during the last thirty years might well be summed up in a title such as: 'Fings ain't what they used to be'.

(a) *Richard II* (Shakespeare). John of Gaunt's speech in Act II, Scene I.
    From 'This land of such dear souls....
    To 'Hath made a shameful conquest of itself'.
(b) Meeting of local Council discussing new by-pass. Unfortunately a block of houses will have to be pulled down

and families and old people will have to be moved and rehoused. They interview an elderly couple who have lived there all their lives and object to the compulsory move.

(c) Committee agrees expenditure of $2\frac{1}{2}$ million pounds on road works. Next business – application for clothing grant of £5 for poor youth called Timothy Winters. Grant not allowed.

(d) *Timothy Winters* (Charles Causley).

(e) From a Local Authority pamphlet on Sand and Gravel extraction: 'Few of the roads and bridges within the study area were constructed with the present traffic levels and tyres in mind and consequently there are considerable traffic problems, particularly in the villages.'

'Gravel working often leads to loss of good quality agricultural land.'

'The sand and gravel companies are concerned to ensure that their stock of land with planning permission is sufficient to meet sudden changes in demand and to make long-term investment decisions.'

(f) From *Watership Down* (Richard Adams) Chapter 2.
'Hazel, the danger, the bad thing ... I don't think he'll like the idea at all.'
'Well, Sir,' said Hazel ... Hazel held him down with his forepaws and he grew quieter.'

(g) From *English Journey* (J. B. Priestley) Chapter 4, Page 86.
'Possibly what I was seeing was not Birmingham but ... and dreariness and ugliness.'

(h) From *Hymn on Morning of Christ's Nativity* (John Milton) Stanzas 13, 14 and 15. 'Ring out, ye crystal spheres' *to* 'Will open wide the gates of her high palace hall'.

These excerpts should give sufficient stimulus to groups to encourage research to find more material on this theme. The excerpts can be linked by comment, music or song.

Marching as to War

Improvisation

This theme provides opportunity to express conflict, love and hate, cruelty, forgiveness and sacrifice.

Inevitably, young people want to explore the great problem of conflict between men. The cruelty and sorrow of War are all too apparent, and yet it has its attractions of uniforms, discipline, self-sacrifice and heroism. Not least, War seems to inspire singable songs. The successful musical show, *Oh, it's a lovely War*, is, to a great extent, an example of extended improvisation.

(a) *Henry V.* (Shakespeare) Act III, Scene 1.
'Once more into the breach....'
(b) Book of Common Prayer. 'Collect for Peace'.
(c) *Bayonet Charge* (Ted Hughes)
(d) *Disabled* (Wilfred Owen) First and last verses.
(e) *Charge of the Light Brigade* Extract verses on valour.
(f) *Murder in the Cathedral* (T. S. Eliot) Speech of the Third Knight.
'I am afraid I am not ... *to*
I think that is about all I have to say.'
(g) Sir Winston Churchill: 'Blood, sweat and tears' speech.
(h) *Dooley is a Traitor* (James Michie)
'So then you won't fight' *to* 'no joke to laugh at after'.
(i) *On the Thirteenth Day of Christmas* (Charles Causley).

Again the group will find their own excerpts to make the points they have in mind. These extracts can be linked with music or songs such as:

British Grenadiers
Will ye no come back again?
Where have all the flowers gone?

'You Said It'

An Easter Play

NOEL: A quiet, scholarly boy, kindly and capable.

JUDE: Something of a rebel, quick-tempered and jealous of Noel's command.

PETER: Noel's greatest admirer who works on Noel's ideals and ideas.

TOM: Just a bit slow in understanding but firm when his mind is made up.

MAGDA Very fond of Noel and follows him around unashamedly.

MARTHA Always organising something.

MARIA The prayerful one, somewhat contemplative.

Other members of the youth club.

THE SCENE The Youth Club. The setting must give the impression of newness. One or two comfortable chairs in one corner balance a table with more practical chairs in one part of the room. Suggest the comfort and style of the club with a pleasant drape or two, some appropriate pictures and a club notice board.

Tom and Peter come in with Magda and Maria. They sit about, trying out chairs and looking at the fittings.

PETER Just look at this room – it's great, it's comfortable and we can really feel that we have a clubroom at last, instead of that grotty old barn of a place we used to put up with.

TOM Yeah, and it's all due to Noel. I didn't think we could do it when he first told us what he meant the club to be. He got that grant from the council and then got us doing all sorts of things to raise money. You wouldn't think that such a brainy chap could be so practical.

MAGDA I knew he could do it. He could make people do anything he wanted them to. He is so quiet and yet so forceful. I've never known anyone like him.

TOM And you've had a few boy friends in your time. Is he your steady boy now?

MAGDA I don't know, it's hard to tell. He seems to be everyone's boy and yet belongs to no one. I wish he was mine.

MARIA I know just how you feel. He's so kind in his quiet way yet somehow he's remote. I can't see him ever making any girl his regular partner.

PETER Well, he's certainly made this a grand place. We ought to be getting some sort of programme out.

TOM We don't want to be too organised. Most of us just like being here, playing table-tennis, billiards and darts; an evening or two of disco and after that, just being here. There's a grand kitchen through there and we could have coffee and things every night with a fry-up of sausages or hamburgers on special nights.

MAGDA I think Noel wants to arrange one or two definite things like play-readings and study nights as well as the usual fun. I know he wants us to start some work which helps other people, poor children and old folk. We have to be outward-looking.

PETER I'm not sure that will be popular.

Enter Jude.

Hello, Jude, come on in. Isn't this great? We're just discussing club activities. What do you think?

JUDE This is fine, much better than I thought it would be. Noel and Martha are just coming in. They've got some ideas about what we ought to do.

Noel and Martha and other members come in and sit around on chairs, on the floor, etc.

NOEL Well, this does look good. Welcome everyone to our new-look club. It's just what I'd hoped it would be. Any ideas about the club and its future?

PETER Well, we've just been talking about activities and apart from the usual club nights with coffee, coke, games and disco, we thought you might like to have a few sessions on more serious topics.

NOEL Yes, that sounds reasonable. I would like us to spend a bit of time thinking about other people, less well-off than we are. Some of us could go down to the children's home now and again and entertain and play with the kids.

MARTHA I like that, and we could occasionally have money-raising events for the old folk and the hospital. We might now and again link up with the church or chapel when they have that kind of function.

JUDE That sounds a bit serious doesn't it? Surely our club is for us to have fun in. We need a place like this to get away from our homes and kid brothers and so on and enjoy ourselves.

MAGDA I think we can cover both the fun and the more serious things, but tonight is for fun.

NOEL I am sure we can work this out. I do want the club to be something more than a place to play about in. Let's have a good time here as well as trying to help in the community outside. After all, we did get a lot of help from outside to realise our dream of a club of our own.

MARIA Good, that's settled. Now who's going to help make tea and coffee. I've brought stuff for a few sandwiches and a cake that needs cutting up. Some on, any volunteers?

All go out except Jude, Peter and three or four other members.

JUDE If Noel has his way, we'll soon be singing psalms. I thought the club was for our benefit, not the old codgers down in the almshouses.

PETER Noel doesn't want to stop our fun, but he's right to point out other responsibilities.

JUDE You would stick up for him. Well, I'm disappointed, and I can't say I agree with you. Come on lads, who's for a game of cards?

Agreement from some of the others who settle with Jude round a table.

MEMBER What shall we play? Rummy?

ANOTHER MEMBER That's a bit soft isn't it? Let's have a game of Solo or something.

Some agree, others make other suggestions.

JUDE Quiet, you lot. Let's put a bit of spice in it. What about Pontoon, with a five-penny limit. We'll play for pennies so no one can lose too much.

PETER You know, I don't think Noel would like that – not gambling for money. Play for counters or matchsticks if you must gamble, but there's always trouble when you play for money.

JUDE Oh, do shut up, school teacher. Anyone would think Noel was God the way you talk. It's our club isn't it, and we can do what we want. Come on lads, out with your money.

The game starts – it gets a bit rowdy. Peter is troubled as he looks on.
Enter Noel at a point where the players are argumentative.

NOEL (*angry*) What do you lot think you're doing. (*He strides across and tips the table over.*) I didn't work for this club so that you could turn it into a gambling den.

Shouts from Jude and members.

JUDE You think you can boss everyone around but we're members too. Why should you make all the rules. There's nothing wrong in playing cards.

NOEL (*quietly*) There's nothing wrong in playing cards, but I do object to members playing for money. For one thing not everyone can afford to play for money, and gambling only leads to greed and envy. I could not remain connected with the club if we start that sort of thing. I'd sooner see it destroyed. It must stand for things that are good and not things that are corrupt.

PETER Noel's right, you know. The club will get a bad name if it does not aim at high standards of behaviour. Then we'd lose the support of the council and all the other people who contributed.

JUDE It's not fair – the club is for our enjoyment and if we want to gamble I think we should be able to. (*Some support from members.*) I know what you want to do here, Noel, but I think you're wrong. You don't think I'd be the one to wreck your ideas, do you?

NOEL Well, you said it. However, for the time being I must stop it. We'll put it to our committee and then members must stick to their ruling.

Noel, Peter and some members go out.

MEMBER It's not fair, Jude. I reckon you ought to be leader of the club – you're not soft like that Noel.

Agreement from members who have stayed.

ANOTHER MEMBER I bet most of the club will choose Noel and the place will be run like a Sunday School. I'm not staying if that happens. What about you, Jude?

JUDE I'd like to stay and in fact I was one of Noel's supporters when we started on the new club. But he's disappointed me and I don't like being let down. I feel like burning the place down.

MEMBER You can't do that, Jude, not after all the work we've done.

Call from other room: 'Coffee up – come and get it!'
All go but Jude.

JUDE It's all a big let-down. Noel's too soft and I'm never coming back to the club. I feel so mad that I could tear the place apart. That's an idea! I'll do it tonight and leave enough evidence to throw the blame on Noel. A lot of us heard him say that he'd sooner see the club destroyed if we didn't want to do as he says. I'll do it, tonight. (*Exit*)

Pause to denote passage of time – lower lights, if any, are used.
Jude enters and methodically overturns table, mimes the actions of destroying furniture and furnishings, leaving the place ransacked.
Pause to denote passage of time.

Peter, Tom, Magda, Martha, Maria enter dejectedly and sit about where they can.

PETER I can't believe that Noel could have done all this. He loved the place, why should he want to wreck it?

TOM But you said yourself, that he said he'd sooner see it wrecked than go the wrong way. And there was the evidence of his own pocket wallet among the wreckage.

MARTHA And how do we get over the fact that he was here when the police were called?

MAGDA I believe him when he says that he got a telephone call and came to see what was happening. He doesn't know who it was because the voice was disguised.

MARIA But if he had only just got here, how did his wallet get underneath the glass from the picture that was smashed?

TOM That's a puzzle. What worries me is that the police are holding him for so long. This is the third day of his arrest. Surely if they weren't satisfied they couldn't keep him all this time.

PETER Yes, that's very worrying. I feel real bad that I was the one to give him away. I didn't realise that my statement that he had said he would rather see the place destroyed would be taken that way.

MARTHA The other thing that has surprised me is the estimate of the damage done. The police had to act with so much involved.

MAGDA Well, we can't sit around here moping. We ought to do something.

MARIA There's not much we can do, but sit around and hope.

Noel enters.

MAGDA Noel – is it really you?

NOEL Yes, it's me.

TOM I can't believe it. You really here. No police escort. Are you sure you're not a ghost?

NOEL Touch me if you like. I'm real enough.

PETER But what happened – have the police charged you?

NOEL No, they haven't. It appears that one of our members saw Jude coming into the club earlier and when he came out he looked very suspicious, so the chap followed him. He went to a telephone box and talked into the mouthpiece with a bit of his handkerchief over it. He's confessed that it was he who did the damage and tried to blame it on to me.

MARIA What's happened to him? Are the police going to arrest him?

NOEL They will when they get him, but he's run away. We won't see him in the club any more.

PETER Well, everything's all right then. We can go on with the club when the mess is cleared up with Noel as club leader.

NOEL (*quietly*) I'm afraid that won't be possible. When I was arrested, before I went into a cell, I had to be medically examined. I haven't been too well lately and it seems there's something very wrong.

MAGDA Whatever do you mean? Will you have to go to hospital?

NOEL Hospital won't help, I'm afraid. It's too serious for that. They say I'm likely to die. They were very definite about it.

Astonishment and dismay shown by all.

MAGDA Oh, no! It can't be. You will get better.

NOEL I am afraid I won't. I'm not surprised, strangely enough.

TOM Well, it can't be too bad – you'll be leader of the club for a long time yet. We'll do all the work while you take it easy. We can't do without you, you know.

NOEL I'm afraid you will have to. They say I've got about a month, forty days at the most. I'll do all I can in that time, but after that you will be on your own. I want you to take over the leadership, Peter. You know just how things should go and I know I can trust you. You'll have to be a kind of foundation for the new club to be built on.

MARTHA It doesn't seem possible, but if you say so, it will have to be. While you are with us, set us on the right lines. After that, as you say, it will be up to us, and we must see that the club is run just the way you wanted it. If our work is well done, the club will still be running for many years ahead.

This playlet may be acted out by a group of young people or used for a play reading. It is not intended as a play for public presentation but a basis for discussion.

Using the events in the play, it is possible to draw out the parallels with the Easter Story and lead to a closer study of the events of Holy Week, Easter Day and Ascension Day, as they are described in the New Testament.

Christ Is Risen

An Improvisation on the Easter Message

Source material from which to choose items that will form a woven pattern to express the Christian joy which springs from an appreciation of the message of Christ's Passion and Resurrection.

MUSIC

Hymn. *O Sacred Head sore wounded.*
Sans Day Carol. *Now the holly bears a berry.*
Sussex Mummers' Carol. *O mortal man, remember well.*
Carol. *Cheer up, friends and neighbours.*
Select passages from *The Messiah.* (Handel).
'Morning'. *Peer Gynt Suite* (Grieg).
'Nimrod'. *Enigma Variations* (Elgar).
Scherzo. *Eroica* Symphony (Beethoven).
Carol. *Now glad of heart be everyone.*

DRAMA

Christ in the concrete city. P. W. Turner.
A Man dies. Hooper and Marvin.
Man born to be King. Dorothy Sayers.
Who was he? D. H. Lawrence.

POETRY

The Killing. Edwin Muir.
Easter. Edmund Spenser.
Ballad of the Bread Man. Charles Causley.

PROSE

The Jerusalem Bible.
Matthew, Chapters 16, 17, 21, 26, 27, 28.
Mark, Chapters 11, 14, 15, 16.
Luke, Chapters 19, 22, 24.
John, Chapters 12, 20, 28.

Use all the techniques of speech, song, mime, dance, movement and drama to express what you feel about the Christian season between Good Friday and Easter.

Book List

Drama and Education, A. F. Alington, Blackwell, London.

Teaching Mime, Rose Bruford, Methuen, London.

Stories of the Hindus, James Kirk, Macmillan, London.

Sacred Tales of India, Nath Neogi, Macmillan, London.

Music for Mime, Barbara Lander, Methuen, London.

Choral Verse, Alexander Franklin, Oliver & Boyd, Edinburgh.

Handbook for Modern Educational Dance, Valerie Preston, McDonald & Evans, Plymouth.

Goalkeeper's Revenge and other stories (*Spit Nolan*), Bill Naughton, Penguin Books, London.

Sound and Sense, Wilton Cole, Allen & Unwin, London.

Improvisation, Hodgson and Richards, University Press.

Tie and Dye, Anne Maile, Mills and Boon, London.

Dyeing and Printing, Marshall Cavendish, London

Come, Holy Spirit, Peter de Rosa, Fontana, London.

Timothy Winters (Contemporary Poetry set to Music), Charles Causley, Turret Books, London.

Voice, G. Summerfield (Ed.), Penguin, London.

Junior Voices, G. Summerfield (Ed.), Penguin, London.

Music Suitable for Dance Themes

Working Music, *Factory*, Mossolov.
    Pictures at an Exhibition, Mussorgsky.
Storm Music, *The Flying Dutchman Overture*, Wagner.
    Selection from *6th Symphony*, Beethoven.
    Grand Canyon, Grofe.
    Sinfonia Antarctica, Vaughan Williams.
Fights and Battle, Selection from *Romeo and Juliet*,
    Tchaikowsky.
    Battle of the Huns, Liszt.
Market and busy scenes, *Pictures at an Exhibition*,
    Mussorgsky.
    London Symphony, Vaughan Williams.
    Street Corner Overture, A. Rowsthorne.
    My Fair Lady (Market Scene), Lerner.
    Cries of London (*Oliver*), Bart.
Religious Themes, *Mass in B. Minor*, Bach.
    Requiem, Faure.
    Requiem, Verdi.
    Symphony of Sounds, Stravinsky.
Dream Theme, *Après midi d'un Faune*, Debussy.
    Cold Winter, Sibelius.
    Pavane pour une infante defunte, Ravel.
Fire and Flames, *Prince Igor Dances*, Borodin.
    Ritual Fire Dance, De Falla.
Mystery and Magic, *Scheherezade*, Rimsky Korsakov.
    Sorcerer's Apprentice, Dumas.
    The Planets, Holst.

Index